LAND
INVESTMENT
U.S.A.

OTHER BOOKS BY LELAND FREDERICK COOLEY
AND LEE MORRISON COOLEY

The Simple Truth about Western Land Investment
The Retirement Trap
How to Avoid the Retirement Trap

NOVELS BY LELAND FREDERICK COOLEY
(Member, Authors League of America)

The Run for Home
God's High Table
The Richest Poor Folks
The Trouble with Heaven
Condition Pink

LAND INVESTMENT U.S.A.

By Leland Frederick Cooley and
Lee Morrison Cooley

Nash Publishing, Los Angeles

Library of Congress Catalog Card Number: 72-95252
International Standard Book Number: 0-8402-1313-1

Published simultaneously in the United States and Canada
by Nash Publishing Corporation, 9255 Sunset Boulevard,
Los Angeles, California 90069.

Printed in the United States of America.

First Printing.

This book is for Lew and Ann

Acknowledgments

In the preparation of this book the authors traveled many thousands of miles and talked with scores of people who were more than generous with their time.

We have reviewed our research notes, our tapes, and our correspondence in an effort to acknowledge their help and give our thanks to everyone who made a substantive contribution to this work. But with so many contacts in so many places, it seems inevitable that some lapses will occur.

If it proves to be the unhappy case that such omissions were made, it was wholly inadvertent and we sincerely regret them; they should imply no lack of gratitude.

The Authors

Our thanks, then, to: Keith B. Abel, Vice President in charge of sales, Lakeway, Texas. Charles D. Allis, President, Sunriver Properties, Inc., Sunriver, Oregon. John N. Bailey, Executive Director, Western Developers Council. R. B. Beck, Southeastern Division Manager, Southern California Edison Co. John E. Black, Real Estate Commissioner, State of Oregon. Hu Blonk, Managing Editor, *Wenatchee World*, Wenatchee, Washington. Betty Brandt, Secretary, Land O'Lakes Chamber of Commerce, Wisconsin. Russell F. Bright, B. J. Lerner & Co., Inc. Robert P. Burbank, Manager,

Huntington Beach, Southern California Edison Co. Carl Burlingame, Publisher, *Recreation Land and Leisure Housing Report.* Rod Campbell, President, Incline Village Realty, Incline Village, Nevada. Gloria Chadwick, Vice President, Director of Marketing, Big Sky, Montana. Mrs. Charmaine Crown, Director, Consumer Protection Division, Office of the Attorney General, State of New Mexico. Prall Culviner, Vice President, Edison Electric Institute, New York. Charles Detoy, Administrative Vice President for Career Division, Colwell Banker, Los Angeles. George L. Dymesich, Land Estate Planner, Cottonwood, California. William Franklin, ADSCO Properties, Tucson, Arizona. Marion Geoble, Executive Secretary, Lake County Chamber of Commerce, Lakeport, California. Paul E. Gregg, Sr., Gregg Realty, Kelseyville, California. Gordon Griffith, Rancho California, Kaiser-Aetna Corp. Ed Haefner, Sales Department, Kino Springs, Kincoa Corp., Boston, Massachusetts. Matt Hammond, Tyrolian Village, Incline Village, Nevada. Lew Harding, Fountain Hills, Arizona, McCulloch Corporation. Don Hargen, Fairfield Green Valley Inc., Arizona. John Heimann, Steele Park Resort, Lake Berryessa, California. Mike Hendrix, General Sales Manager, Pine Mountain Club, Tenneco Inc. Wesley H. Hillendahl, Vice President, Bank of Hawaii. Richard Hobson, North American Towns of Texas. Betsy Hodges, Research Director, Orlando Area Chamber of Commerce, Orlando, Florida. "Pete" Hollick, Assistant Executive Officer, Tahoe Regional Planning Agency. A. Garner House, Sales Department, Carefree Developers, Inc., Carefree, Arizona. Thomas R. Jordan, President, Underwood, Jordan Associates, New York, N.Y. "Jim" Journigan, President, La Jolla Land & Cattle, Scottsdale, Arizona. James R. Kane, General Manager, Lakeway World of Tennis, Lakeway, Texas. Donna Kelly, Public Relations, Sunriver, Oregon. William Kirircher, East Central Florida Regional Planning Council, Orlando, Florida. Ray Knisely, Special Adviser to Governor O'Callaghan, Carson City, Nevada. Ronald L. Lettenmaier, Black Butte Ranch Corp., Black Butte, Oregon. Robert G. Lucas, Lucas & Meyer, Santa Ana, California. D. J. McFarland, President, Lake Berryessa Development Corporation, California. Walter E. MacKenzie, Manager, Public Information, Sierra Pacific Power Company, Reno, Nevada. N. K. Mendelsohn, President, North American Towns, Inc. Pat Murphy, Manager, Lake Nacimiento Park, Paso Robles, California. National Better Business Bureaus, Incorporated, New York, N.Y. Clifford T. Nutt, Inc. Motor Home Sales, Newport Beach, California. George Oakes, Administrator, Real Estate Division, state of Washington. Tom Parmenter, Sales Representative, Sunriver Properties, Inc., Sunriver, Oregon. David Peters, President, David A. Peters & Associates for Tenneco & Pine Mountain Club, California. Forrest Pettygrew, Assistant Real Estate Commissioner, state of Arizona. H. L. Remmers, San Juan Capistrano & Laguna Niguel, California. Bob Robertson, Diablo East Marina, Lake Amistad, Texas. "Chuck" Rogers, Division Manager, Heritage Ranch, Lake Nacimiento, California. Don Scanlin, Project Manager, The Groves, Amberton, California. Charles Schank, Sales Department, Lake California, Anderson, California. David Schell, Lakeworld, Dart Industries, Los Angeles, California. Andrew R. Schmidt, Planning Team Leader, United States Forest Service, Lake Tahoe, California. Jay A. Serra, Public Relations, Outdoor Resorts of America, Nashville, Tennessee. William C. Smith III, Director of Membership Services, Lakeway World of Tennis, Lakeway, Texas. Lon R. Stark, Executive Vice President, Alpert Investment Corporation, Lakeway, Texas. James Swingley, Sales Representative, La Costa Sales Corp., La Costa, California. J. Fred Talley, Commissioner, State Real Estate Department, Phoenix, Arizona. Byron D. Varner, Off-Site Sales, Lakeway, Texas. Vermont State Real Estate Commission. Jo Vincelette, Public Relations, Trimont Land Corp., Northstar, California. Stanley Weiss, Vice President, North American Towns of California. Chapman Wentworth, Wentworth & Associates, Incline Village, Nevada. Bruce A. Werlhof, Sacramento, California. Val Williams, Lake Shastina, Weed, California. Holly Wilson, Wentworth & Associates, Incline Village, Nevada. Barbara Wright, Futura Mobile Home Sales, U. S. Financial Group, Oceanside, California. Howard Van Lente, Project Manager, Riviera Heights, Clear Lake; Custom Properties, Inc., San Francisco, California. Michael Zarro, Director of Sales, La Costa, California.

Contents

LAND
INVESTMENT
U.S.A.

1.
For Land's Sake

In 1867, English novelist Anthony Trollope wrote, "It is a very comfortable thing to stand on your own ground." If he had stopped there he would have stated a generally accepted fact. But being a novelist, he could not resist a bit of innocent fiction so he added, "Land is the only thing that can't fly away."

If Trollope had studied a little basic geography and geology he would have known that land can and does "fly away." Parts of the Sahara Desert were once rich agricultural areas. So were parts of the sweltering, oil-rich Near Eastern region from which, it is said, came the cedar planks for Noah's Ark and for the furniture, barges, chariots and whatnot of countless Egyptian dynasties.

Long ago armies of "ologists" proved that our own great southwestern desert was once a lush tropical paradise; and certainly the survivors of the great Dust Bowl tragedy of the late 1920s and early 1930s can tell us that land does, indeed, fly away—quite literally—and its value with it.

More recently, though, it is not an act of God that makes land values "fly away." It is the avarice of man himself. A century ago the census showed 13.4 Americans per square mile of land. By 1970, 54.4 Americans were living on each square mile of land despite the fact that we had added some 1,609,277 square miles of land through the acquisition of new states and territories. In only one hundred years our population had risen from 40 million to 203 million, and by the next census, in 1980, we shall number about 233 million Americans. Project that growth rate to 1985 and our "head count" will be *one-quarter of a billion Americans.*

Since we are not a militant nation given to territorial conquest, it is unlikely that we will acquire significant amounts of new national real estate. And since there are more and more of us crowding onto our limited available land, we must take a careful look at how we are using this most basic of natural resources. That is what the conservationists and the ecologists are urging us to do. And well should we heed the warnings of the rational voices among them.

We in the United States face a number of urgent challenges. Some are social and some are economic, and it seems odd that many experts insist upon separating them. To us, they appear to be inextricably related as socio-economic problems.

We have an energy crisis—a very real one. But we cannot get large numbers of people excited about it, and we probably won't until it affects every American home. We have a water crisis in large areas of the country, either because we have expanded our population into water-short areas or because we have polluted the once bountiful supply at hand. The Great Lakes and the great midcontinental rivers are prime examples. But we do not get too excited about that either even though the conservationists have sounded their alarms for a decade or more. Only in recent years—in the past three or four—have we begun to understand the dangers inherent in continued air pollution. And still, such are the vagaries of human nature that our concern about cleaning up the land, the air and the water, often has more to do with protecting profits than with preserving people.

Charles Dudley Warner, the distinguished New England author-editor who occasionally collaborated with his neighbor Mark Twain, wrote in 1870, "To own a bit of ground, to scratch it with a hoe, to plant seeds, and watch the renewal of life—this is the commonest delight of the race, the most satisfactory thing a man can do."

Why? Because next to the procreation of his own species, man's highest-priority obligation is the initiation and preservation of those other forms of the life miracle that will sustain the human family. In short, man's second duty is the protection and the highest and best use of his particular "bit of ground." And that is why, among all investments, land has always been, and quite probably always will be, *man's most fundamental investment.*

Our civilization has become so complex in the last century that not everybody can discharge that primary obligation directly. Millions of city dwellers are denied their own private piece of the good earth on which they can sustain and recreate themselves. But it seems safe to say that few mortals do not respond to such a basic desire—even if it means settling for a pot of geraniums, an African violet or a kitchen window "garden" of chives.

We have seen that since 1870 the number of Americans per mile of land has increased by four times—from 13.4 to 54.4— even though our country has grown by no more than a half million square miles.

Quite simply, those figures mean that for each of us, theoretically, the parcel of land we do have has become four times more desirable—or four times more "valuable" in the sense that in a situation where we have a *permanently fixed supply of land,* four times as many people need the use of it in one form or another. And so we come face to face with the principal marketplace value factor—the law of supply and demand.

In purely agrarian civilizations, the possession of that personal or communal piece of "Mother Earth" was a matter of life and death in its simplest terms. Local, regional, national and finally global wars have been fought over the possession of productive land.

When the male half of this writing team was a young journalist in Italy in April of 1936, Mussolini, addressing a group of us, said, "What you Americans do not understand is this—Italy has a population of 50 million people living in an area less than the size of California. We must have Ethiopia or starve!" If that sounds familiar, it is no wonder, for it is the same argument used first by Kaiser Wilhelm and later by Hitler to rationalize the policy of Lebensraum; and by the Japanese jingoists to justify their Asian expansion policy in the late 1930s.

In military terms, supremacy of the sea and the air simply meant a crucial advantage in the greater strategy to protect (or conquer) land. Who can count the millions who have died on the battlefields in the name of land?

In the sweat of thy face shalt thou eat bread, till thou return unto the ground; for out of it wast thou taken: for dust thou art, and unto dust shalt thou return. . . .

It was man's intuitive understanding of his sacred bond to the land that inspired those nameless ancients to set down in Holy Scripture man's relationship to God and His land. But what has happened to land and man's relationship to it in modern times has little to do with holiness and almost wholly to do with cupidity.

As a fundamental investment then, land has no equal, for the roots of our security lie deep in well-chosen, well-used land.

In the following chapters we will attempt to show the non-professional buyer how to choose a land investment from among the many options available and, more importantly, how to avoid the "land butchers" and "paradise peddlers" whose promises of instant fortunes assail our eyes and ears in the press, on radio and on television, twenty-four hours a day, seven days a week. Only the tax collector is more relentless in his pursuit of our hard-won dollars.

1. Once this was an area of beautiful, gently rolling hills covered with poppy and lupine along Southern California's coast. Now, this cut-and-fill technique of "land development" has turned most of California's hill country into a series of shelf-like tracts. Much lip service is paid to conservation and preservation and esthetic values, but, in the end, the "highest and best" use of land is determined by the maximum number of tract houses that can be squeezed in per acre.

2. *A natural slope with nature's built-in safeguards against erosion has been sliced into a compacted incline. Later ice plant and other alien ground cover will be planted to accomplish, in part, what natural cover on natural slopes did with efficiency and beauty. A sad paradox—in Southern California, we "customize" the land so we can "mass produce" the housing . . . the complete reverse of the beautiful logic practiced at Lakeway, Texas.*

2.
Investment Objectives

"I just want a piece of land of my own—out away from things. I don't give a damn where it is—I just want the comfort of knowing that I've got a piece of ground that is mine—a place I can run to."

The statement was made by a Chicago "inner city" executive as we sat in his elegant lakefront condominium. A lot of things had happened to trigger the reaction. There was an undertone of urgency—a sense of impending peril that had brought the man close to panic. Emotion was overriding his usual sound judgment.

Only a few days earlier there had been a horrible commuter train accident. Several of his employees had been involved. A few weeks earlier, the local courts had set free some political activists who, our friend sincerely believes, are dedicated to the overthrow of the things he has devoted a lifetime to building. He suddenly felt trapped. The pro rata portion of the huge skyscraper condominium that he owned did not satisfy his need to have a secure place of his own. To quote him further, "Here I'm just another pigeon in the cote—and a sitting pigeon at that! What I want is a little farm."

In Cleveland, we visited forty-three-year-old George Huntinger and his wife, Emma. For eighteen years George has worked in a metal-fabricating plant. Those years have been spent in pandemonium amidst the clank of giant stamping machines, the shrieking protests of heavy metal unwillingly bent and the deafening, blinding electric crackle of banks of arc welders. When George leaves the plant at four in the afternoon he drives through bumper-to-bumper traffic—a good part of the year in foul weather—to a modest single-family residence.

His neighborhood is gradually changing from lower-middle-class working whites to an area of mixed Americans in the same relative economic bracket. "My Archie Bunker house," George calls his place. "I don't mean the wife and I don't get along with our new neighbors. It's just that—well—it's different here now. It's not relaxed like it was. I got no beef with my neighbors. And sure as hell I'm not going to move away, like some. But Emma and I are looking for a place where we can spend our vacations—like two or three hours out in the country, and maybe long weekends—just so we can settle down inside ourselves. Nothing fancy. Just a little place to put up a prefab."

An airline captain friend of ours, who lived in Newport Beach, California, a beautiful, yachting-oriented community, found his retreat in a fashionable condominium in the Colorado Rockies. A few miles to the north, in the new, sprawling suburban community of Fountain Valley—once one of California's richest agricultural centers—master mechanic Harold Anderson and his wife, Mary, found their retreat in a well-designed mobile home court from which they make excursions all over the western United States and Canada.

In New York City, Frances Herridge, movie and drama editor of the *New York Post,* and her theatrical-producer husband, Adna Karns, have found their "retreat" on fourteen acres of beautifully wooded slope in Woodstock, New York. When we visited the once secluded area we found that hundreds of other urbanites had also discovered Woodstock.

On Islamorada Key in Florida, a Midwestern conglomerate executive found his retreat in a modest waterfront cottage. "I've gone from mergers to mullet," he laughs. "The only thing I try to put together down here is a fishing pole—and I'm beginning to think that activity is actually paying me the biggest dividends!"

In Burlington, Vermont, a working couple bought two lots in a Florida Gulf Coast development. They will not be able to build for five years when their lots will be fully improved. But they took the predevelopment "bargain" because it will be their retirement home site seven years hence.

Our taped and handwritten notes gathered in every state but Alaska (to get away from it all up there you just step out the back door) are eloquent evidence of the change in our American life-style—of the discontent that millions are beginning to feel as the old order and the old values change.

An articulate young attorney in San Francisco put it this way: "That Horatio Alger bit is a lot of crapola. The real American Tragedy is not knocking up the neighbor girl and dumping her out of the canoe. It's spending your life chasing the almighty buck.

"I'm moving my practice up to a little town you never heard of. I can pan for gold in the backyard and catch my breakfast there too. In duck season it's just one hour down to the rice fields in the valley; and in deer season I can shoot a buck from my back porch. And, by the way, that's the only buck worth chasing."

His bride of fourteen months agrees. "Bruce and I want the same things," she said. When we asked if they would not feel isolated they looked at us incredulously. "Isolated? With television and radio? With the city (San Francisco) only two hours away—with good plays, opera, art galleries? . . . We are really into another way of life now. Who in hell needs a million dollars? You know, after the tax collector and the head shrinker you wind up a pauperized basket case. My old man went that route. For us? No way."

The one thing these young Americans and the scores of others of all ages to whom we spoke had in common was the desire to "get away from it all." With very few exceptions, they wanted "a place to go"—a retreat where they could find relief from the pressure of urban and suburban living.

Only two decades ago the urbanites found such relief by fleeing to the suburbs. As our population increased and expressways, parkways and freeways proliferated into a great concrete net, even the suburbanites found themselves trapped. It is their renewed desire to get still further away from it all that has sparked the greatest land boom our country has seen.

Keenly sensitive to new markets that can add to their millions, a clutch of huge corporations, many never before associated with land development, have bought up hundreds of thousands of acres of our most beautiful wilderness and waterfront and are now in the process of carving it up into recreational and second-home subdivisions.

Too often, the consequences to the affected areas are catastrophic. Always they are considerable. Later on, when we discuss the ecological and economic reactions to this sort of subdivision, we shall cite some good and some bad examples of land usage and the effects they have upon long-term investment values.

Meanwhile, the purpose of this chapter is to raise the primary question that every investor should ask: *What is my real reason in wishing to invest in a parcel of land?*

Do I want a quiet, safe retreat from the pressures of urban living—a second home I can take my family to on weekends or on holidays and vacations?

Do I want to become an exurbanite, or perhaps, an "ex*sub*urbanite"—establish my principal home in the uncrowded "boondocks" and commute to work—or make my home my office?

Do I want to become a gentleman farmer and work some acreage—return or retreat to the simple pastoral joys of growing and harvesting food for my own table?

Do I want to acquire some land on which I can develop a second home that eventually will become my principal residence when I retire?

Do I want to acquire some inexpensive raw land for purely recreative purposes—a place to take my camper and get away from it all?

Do I want to gamble on some remote, inexpensive raw land in the "path of progress" to hold simply for speculation? If so, can I afford to hold it for ten years or more?

Do I want to buy improved property in a good development as an investment holding?

Those are some basic questions you must ask yourself.

Few investments offer such a broad spectrum of possibilities as land. Purchases may range from a two-and-one-half acre plot of "jackrabbit" land in the general area we call "West Hellangone" in our first land investment book* to an office building site at the corner of Broadway and Main that is purchased by the square inch.

But even the least sophisticated purchase requires some basic knowledge on the buyer's part if it is to be a sound investment. With the exception of Real Estate Investment Trusts, we shall exclude the super-sophisticated Real Estate Syndicates that are usually available only to the "big-money boys."

Instead we shall address ourselves to those simpler options that are available to the so-called "average buyer" and which, if they are well chosen, can double or triple in value within a surprisingly short time. More often than one would imagine, well-chosen land, *well used,* can increase in value ten times or more within two decades. We would refer skeptics who challenge that statement to the opening personal anecdote in our earlier book that tells of our own first experience with land investment in 1952 on Suffolk County's famous (sometimes notorious) Fire Island in New York State. For us, that was the eye-opening beginning of an engrossing avocation that has given us the freedom to roam the world and write our books.

The Simple Truth About Western Land Investment, Doubleday, 1964 (revised, 1968).

3.
Success Insurance

Behind every successful investment lies a first principle: *Be certain you know why you wish to invest, investigate the options and then take the time needed to inform yourself about the particular investment you choose.*

The principle applies equally to the gaming tables in Las Vegas and Reno and to "the world's largest permanent floating crap game"—Wall Street. Certainly, it applies to any sort of a real estate investment. And, fortunately for the "average investor," with competent help real estate can be one of the easiest investments to assess correctly. But because of its primordial appeal—man's "territorial imperative"—it may also be one of the easiest investments to make *too quickly.*

Many of the recent books dealing with land investment were written by men and women with axes to grind. Usually they are brokers or promoters or developers, people directly related to the real estate industry by way of syndicates and "trust." They are, perforce, special pleaders. Most of them are practitioners of a new sales science we have dubbed "euphemology." They are masters in the art of mental imagery—"paradise peddlers" and "mirage merchants"—people who have developed the use of the adjective to an exact science that can turn you on to a "Heavenly Homesite" in the heart of Death Valley in July!

In case you are wondering about our particular "ax," let us clarify our positions right here. We are authors, writers, reporters. That is our "thing," as our daughters say. When we are not investigating nonfiction subjects that interest us (and hopefully will interest and be of service to you), the male half of this team writes novels.

How did we get interested in land investment, and why do we feel qualified to speak to the so-called "average investor"? That story is fully told in our first land book, *The Simple Truth about Western Land Investment,* in the chapter entitled, "A Solid Gold Gun at Our Heads."

After years of trying to make sense out of other investments, we were literally dragged, by friends, into a land investment in New York's Suffolk County, and—wonder of wonders—we found that even a harassed television writer-producer and his choreographer wife could understand basic principles. That was twenty-plus years ago, and in all that time no avocation has given us more pleasure and more profit.

We think that it is only fair to say here that twenty years ago land investment was somewhat simpler than it is now. Because of the growing land boom and the understandable concern of ecologists and conservationists, there are many new legal restraints on the parceling and sale of land. That is the reason for this new book.

The "land butchers" among the developers are wailing loudly that their "rights" are being abridged—that they are being put out of business. We, among others, are very happy that some of them are being shut down. In certain Western states we wish they had been put out of business years ago. Unscrupulous land exploiters have done irreparable damage to land values in some areas and have besmirched the ethical professionals as well.

But the pendulum of abuse and reform must always swing to extremes before it finds its point of balance. Because this is true, we often find a tendency to overreaction on the part of some hyperzealous conservationists. In the name of safeguarding the heritage of future Americans, they too have raised havoc with orderly land development.

Several times, in several books, we have pointed out that the safest bet in the world is to bet on human nature. Throughout man's long history, it has performed predictably and unerringly—for good and for bad.

Our democracy has lasted longer than any other because its genius lies in its ability to strike a balance between the extremes of human behavior. And so now we are beginning to see some balance come to the matter of land and its best usages.

If the unethical "developers" (what an extravagant misuse of a good word) had been left unsupervised—unaccountable to anybody but their lenders—it would have taken two generations or more to reverse the damage they might have done in every desirable part of the United States.

But the warnings of the thoughtful conservationists and ecologists are beginning to be heeded all through government at the local, county, state and federal levels. As a consequence, sensibly controlled, carefully planned subdivision and development will eventually result in an increase in land values that was not dreamed of even by the greediest "land butchers."

We could cite a number of happy examples among the new communities and developments springing up around the land. But among the older communities we know of no more heartening example of commonsense restraint than that of Carmel, California, where it takes a city council hearing before a single tree on public property may be disturbed. The protective ordinance was written shortly before World War I when the picturesque little artists' and writers' colony was founded. "Asphalt" is a dirty word, and if you don't like driving around a 200-year-old cypress tree in the middle of the street, then stay out of Carmel.

Everything about the community is planned to insure man's ageless communion with nature; and in the commonsense subordination of his needs to nature's, man has made the remarkable discovery that it is mighty good business too—a fact readily confirmed by anybody who tries to buy a parcel of land in Carmel-by-the-Sea.

"Investigate before you invest," has been the watchword of prudent investors ever since the idea was first voiced back in the time of the Romans when Pliny the Younger counseled a friend to "be certain of the value of the villa and its lands before sending your servant with the gold."

To insure the success of any investment, you need accurate information. If the investment anticipates a long-term increase in value to enhance your eventual capital worth, then you need long-term projections; and the farther they attempt to reach into the future to anticipate coming events, the higher the risk, the wider the margin for error. At some point along such projections a cautious person would have to decide where an investment becomes a speculation. In that case the risk must be calculated together with your willingness to accept it. That would be particularly true in those remote raw-land promotions, mainly in the West and Southwest, that a University of California study calls "Unanchored Subdivisions." By that, the study means land "unanchored to any adjacent urban or suburban development from which, within a reasonable time, the land may draw increased utility and value."

As we get into the various land investment options—the choices open to the average investor—we will discuss more fully the ways in which one can accumulate sound information before making a decision to buy.

Intelligent, persistent questioning is one of the best methods of gathering information. And your questions should not be directed solely to the seller or his agent. After all, when a person wants to dispose of a piece of property, he is tempted to become a special pleader. Very rarely will a seller volunteer information that might be detrimental to the sale. But if you ask for such information and the seller or his agent deliberately misinforms you, then in most cases you will have legal recourse if you have made a purchase. But no amount of legislative safeguards can recover the time you've lost.

If, as Ben Franklin said, "Time is money," then it follows that time well spent in research will pay off in two possible ways—in dollars saved or in dollars earned.

Recently we had good cause to reflect on the wisdom of careful investigation. A ranch in one of our Western states came on the market. We knew the place. It is beautiful. A fine trout stream borders on one side of it, and several small lakes dot the 3,000-plus acres. It was such a desirable piece of property that it was difficult to understand why it should come on the market, particularly in view of the fact that a new highway was about to open up the entire area for recreational development.

We were on the verge of putting a limited partnership together to acquire the place at what seemed a fair price. But as time went on, we learned that the principal was getting more and more anxious to dispose of the holding. The price came down by six figures! And still we needed more time to put our deal together. And thank the Lord, we did!

Just as we were about to fly to the area with the earnest money check in hand, we learned from some random questioning that a huge industry, whose economic "health" affects the entire surrounding area, was about to lose several hundred millions in government work. Several thousand employees would receive their termination notices. As projected, these average wage-earning families would have been our prime prospects for the recreational sites that we planned to develop.

We decided to wait and see, feeling that for every "good deal" that we might lose, another one would surely come along—an important truth to remember.

The government contracts were canceled. Thousands of families did suffer layoffs. Many left the area, simply walking away from small equities in their tract homes. Others found less satisfactory work in the same general area. The economy of hundreds of square miles was severely depressed.

Had we assumed this obligation in the hope that resales would have produced enough cash flow to meet the notes, plus development costs, we would have jeopardized everything we have built up over the years.

In time, the price of the land dropped to about half of its original asking price. Subsequently, it was bought by a diversified corporation that has the resources to hold it until its value returns. The area is improving now. Another three years or so will see it fully recovered. In the meantime, for us, the payments would have been a continuing drain. In the end, we too would have had to sell in distress as the original owner did.

The moral is simple: *There are very few real bargains.*

Instead of sitting around moaning, "Why did we buy it?" we could heave a grateful sigh and say, "Isn't it lucky we took the time to ask one more question?"

It is true that this story is based on a relatively "big deal"— well over a half million dollars in land costs alone. But the same principle applies, even if you are buying a city lot. The only way to insure that you are making a wise investment is to get all of the pertinent information, *not all of which is readily available.*

For example, those people who bought expensive new homes in the suburban developments built to serve the workers in the huge industry we spoke of might well have thought twice about the future of any giant industry that depends almost entirely upon federal defense and aerospace contracts. When things are rolling, it is only human to feel that the boom will last forever. But some of us who remember the Great Depression know better. And subsequent events have proved the truth in the old adage: Those who do not learn from history are doomed to relive its mistakes.

When we counsel friends to search out information, many of them who have no trouble finding out facts pertaining to their own businesses, look at us helplessly and say, "But where do we find out about economic projections? Who is going to tell us what is likely to happen in an area?"

We'll get into the techniques for getting the needed information about the various types of real estate investment in the chapters that deal specifically with each type. But for a general reply, we can think of few better places to go than to the public relations department of your local utility companies.

The electrical companies and the gas companies, and the telephone companies also, do everything they can to take the speculative element out of their own future growth projections. They must borrow hundreds of millions of dollars from the public through bonded indebtedness, and through their bankers, to extend and improve their services. They never run their services out to remote areas in the *hope* that something is going to happen to bring in revenue. They *know* it's going to happen.

Much of their information is quite properly "classified," because if it were to get into the wrong hands unscrupulous speculators in many fields could use it improperly. But with a little digging—discreet questioning of employees that you contact in the course of your daily business—it is possible to pick up a number of valuable clues that can be followed up. A surprising number will prove to have substance.

Again, the point is to get information, and never to stop looking for it. Be on the alert for any sort of news that may have a bearing, positive or negative, on an area that interests you. Conversely, watch the news for new areas that should interest you. In the following chapter you'll find out more about how to watch for valuable investment clues. A good point to remember is this: In land investment as in all other forms of investment, *success insurance* is purchased with time—your time—the time it takes to find out everything possible pertaining to the prospective investment.

Most of us are well aware of the existence of the Better Business Bureaus, but few of us think of them in connection with something as "important" as land investment. And, still, in our research for ways to insure a successful investment in real estate, we found some of the best guidelines of all in the publications of the National Better Business Bureau, Incorporated, 230 Park Avenue, New York City 10017.

In *The Simple Truth About Western Land Investment,* we called their series of questions, "Thirteen Lucky Questions" or "Safeguides." We will be including all of these and a few of our own in subsequent chapters for they make sound good sense. As a matter of fact, we would suggest to anybody wishing to protect his family against the various frauds that are prevalent in the land-sales business that they write to the N.B.B.B. at the above address and request their leaflets on home buying and various other aspects of real estate investment. A lot of "hindsight" and experience has gone into their preparation. There is no such thing as too much "boning up" on this subject!

4.
History—The Investors' 20/20 Hindsight

Behind any investment are a number of basic factors that bear directly on the eventual worth of your purchase. Underlying these factors are historical growth patterns. And in no investment can those patterns be more clearly observed than in the growth and development of real estate values.

But just as one must stand back from a masterpiece to appreciate it fully without being distracted by individual brush strokes, so must one view the history of the growth of an area from a long perspective in order to perceive past basic growth patterns and project them into the future.

Webster's Third New International Dictionary of the English Language (unabridged) defines investment as "the commitment of funds with a view to minimizing risk and safeguarding capital while earning a return—as opposed to speculation."

A broker friend with a flair for grass-roots clarity says, "A speculation is a deal to which the buyer brings some money, a little information and a lot of prayer. An investment is a deal to which the buyer brings some money, a lot of information and a little prayer."

So in the name of well-founded information, let's take a few moments to trace the past growth patterns of our largest urban centers from the present, back to the founding of the first Colonial settlements. If it is true that human nature has undergone no appreciable change since the beginning of recorded time, then it must follow that through an understanding of man's collective past behavior we can increase the possibility of predicting his future performance. With good reason, every handicapper and odds-maker knows that!

When the first shiploads of settlers arrived in the New World, they stepped ashore in sheltered harbors to establish their communities. Into most of those harbors, navigable rivers emptied. In time, as more settlers arrived and the communities grew, the more adventurous among them began to push inland, following the water courses.

Leaving behind the early settlements that had become the first urban communities, these pioneers established camps, usually a day's journey inland. Others, exploring along the coast line, came upon other likely places—other harbors or rich delta lands at the mouths of other rivers—until settlements had been established from what is now the state of Maine all the way down the Atlantic coast.

Those who pushed inland across the mountain barriers found the headwaters of new streams and followed them down to the confluence with still larger streams. There they founded new trading and commercial centers from which other explorers pushed outward along the paths of least resistance, which were the natural roadways formed by navigable streams.

This ageless pattern of migration persisted here as it had in Europe and Asia until all of the easily accessible, logical community sites had been discovered. As the nation's population grew, these new communities grew. With this growth and the beginning of intercommunity commerce, these early Americans needed better and faster means of communication. First came the post roads along the eastern seaboard—the Boston Post Road to New York, the Philadelphia and Baltimore and Washington roads that soon reached down to the nethermost settlements.

Barge canals were financed to connect lakes and rivers. Communities sprang up at logical way points along these man-made shipping channels. Soon the railroads came and more communities developed at rural way points and division points along the lines. Finally, entire populated regions were bound together by a vast network of rails, and the smoke-belching, bell-clanging "Iron Horses" began to pull the United States into a future brighter than the brightest dreams of our wildest visionaries.

Population figures tell the story:

1790	3,929,000	
1800	5,308,000	
1820	9,638,000	(30 years—population
1850	23,192,000	increased 2½ times)
1880	50,156,000	
1900	75,995,000	(In 50 years it tripled)
1910	91,972,000	

And then, in 1920 we broke the 100 million mark— 105,711,000 people, native-born and immigrants, had "discovered America."

Less than a half-century later, by 1968, we had doubled our population. In the last census we numbered 203,235,298 persons*—all sitting on, fighting for or dreaming of their own patch of the "good earth."

In these figures, which are hard facts, lie the first principle of profitable land investment—*people pressure.*** We have increased our population by about 5,000 percent since 1790, but we have increased the available land on which they can live by little more than 400 percent. As Ethel Barrymore said in her famous curtain line, "That's all there is. There isn't any more!" Unless we purchase, or otherwise peaceably acquire, more island

---

*A total of 217,000,000 people is projected for 1975.
**The Cooleys coined the phrase, since generally adopted by demographers and developers here and in Europe. (Ed.)

territory (and their population and problems), we are looking at a *fixed area* into which we must compress another 60 million Americans in the next twenty years.

There is a lot of talk about Zero Population Growth. In some areas of our country, the birthrate has actually declined in the past ten years. But even if we could achieve this *theoretical ideal* nationally, it would take until the year 2040 for our population to level off.

So, no matter what happens in the foreseeable future, "people pressure" will continue to exert its direct force on our society and on our economy, *and particularly on the value of land in the most desirable living areas of the United States.* Later, when we consider recreational land investment, we'll discuss the effects of new leisure time, new mobility and a changing life-style on wilderness areas that only a decade ago were regarded as uninhabitable for all practical purposes.

Three questions are all-important for an investor to ask: What should I buy? Where? And when? They all relate directly to one or more aspects of people pressure. If your primary purpose is a land investment that will appreciate in value in a reasonably short time, then you must learn how to locate these pressure points—how to predict where new ones will develop, and how soon that is likely to happen.

Conversely, if your purpose is to invest in a remote piece of land—to get away from it all—then you will still have to predict where new people pressure points are apt to occur so that you may take advantage of them by *avoiding* them.

In our highly mobile society, an important pressure point can develop almost overnight. A prime example is the Hawaiian Islands. With the advent of the first high-capacity passenger plane, and finally the jumbo jet, all of the amenities of the Islands became available to thousands upon thousands of average Americans whose parents could only dream of visiting a tropical paradise. Fortunes are being made by those who foresaw the influx and bought early.

Those same jumbo jets—the 747s—and soon the "stretch" versions of the DC-10s and Lockheed L-1011s are changing once-remote vacation areas into high-rise jungles all over the globe. Add to them the British-French supersonic Concorde, and the SSTs that we are certain to begin building again, and within a generation there will be no place left to run to. And more fortunes will be made.

As people pressure begins to build up to the point where it threatens the greatest good for the greatest number of people (the conservationists feel we have reached that point now), new controls will certainly be placed on land transactions.

We have seen the beginning of such legislation in the congressional session that ended just prior to the 1972 presidential election.

In response to public concern, the Senate passed a bill—albeit a greatly watered down one—that would allow the federal government to assist states in the development of long-range land use plans. This move completely reverses the classic concept that decisions on land use should lie solely with local government, a principle that often has been badly abused by permissive state and county officials and by unscrupulous exploiters who call themselves land developers.

As of this writing, the House has not acted upon the bill and there is some question that it will. Political observers say that special-interest pressure will probably keep the bill in committee unless public outcry generates sufficient political fear on the part of congressmen to break the impasse. The least cynical among the observers predict that if the bill is passed by the House the end result will be so compromised as to be meaningless—that it will probably be little more than another legal "study boondoggle."

Whatever the outcome on the national level, public concern about the misuse of land is making some sort of realistic control mandatory. In California, against the opposition of powerful special-interest groups, the voters passed Proposition 20, the so-called Coastal Zone Conservation Bill, by a whopping margin despite a heavily financed campaign backed by the real estate, land development and utilities industries.

Complicated and highly restrictive, the act has clamped down all development including the siting of new electrical generating plants, without which the state will inevitably suffer an acute power shortage—some say within three years. In the chapter "Power—Progress or Panic?" we discuss the effect of such a crisis on land values.

It must be clear then that a person wishing to make an investment in land is obliged to do considerably more than drive to locations where new suburbs are building, buy a patch of land out beyond that area, then sit on it and wait to get rich. In the end the prospective investor may come to the conclusion that the jack rabbits, ground hogs, snakes and other critters have more protected rights than he has. The one lesson that history can no longer teach us here in the United States is that we have an unlimited supply of land that we can use and abuse with a prodigal hand without serious consequences to ourselves and to others.

Land values *are* tied to the marketplace—to the law of supply and demand. *Prices are most likely to increase in those areas experiencing the greatest people pressure.* But since those are the first areas to come under the close scrutiny of politicians who themselves are being pressured by environmentalists, there can be some new and kinky local and regional restrictions present that may prejudice the intended use of a particular parcel of land and render it uneconomical.

It follows then that in most states it now becomes more important than ever to *investigate before you invest.* We said earlier that commonsense restriction can actually add to the value of land that is zoned for a particular type of development. But under the onslaught of political pressure, even old zoning can be reversed, sometimes to the detriment of the present owner. We know of two instances where city councils have "down-zoned" commercial beach-front property that was sold to a new owner on the basis of the old, higher density projections. The new purchaser could not prove that the broker knew that new unfavorable zoning was being contemplated. Therefore, he had no recourse but to make the best of a bad bargain.

We know of another area that was down-zoned from single family residences on five acres to the same density on *twenty acres.* Buyers who had purchased to hold until they could build retirement homes were forced to apply for variances or try to acquire adjoining land in order to meet the new minimum rural homesite requirement.

Scaled-down height limits on commercial property have caused expensive plans to be thrown out, created radical downward revisions in cash flow projections and drastic decreases in the profit potential of business and professional buildings.

So, in addition to a working knowledge of the history of a general area and its past growth patterns, a land investor today must also be well informed as to the political climate of the specific area that interests him. To repeat, it is not as simple to make a good land investment today as it was a decade ago when we wrote the first edition of *The Simple Truth about Western Land Investment.*

But, if all the factors are right, we feel that a carefully chosen investment—even a modest and relatively uncomplicated one—now has an even greater potential for profit than ever before.

A person just beginning to get interested in land investment (for all of the new factors, it is still one of the best hedges against inflation) might well ask, "How do we go about studying the past history of an area? And how do we find out about new ordinances and laws that could affect our investment? And how about future plans?"

Clichés and bromides become such because of the simple truths they usually contain. So, once again, *you get out of an effort what you put into it.* And, if you do your work well, you'll get out of a land investment a lot *more* than you put into it.

The general history of any area can be found in an hour or two in the local library. Chances are you already know something about the place anyway—things that first directed your attention there.

The local chamber of commerce will have useful background information. One of the best methods is to leaf through back issues of the local newspaper. Also, subscribe to one if you live elsewhere. It can also be profitable to talk with old established merchants in an area. You may loose a stream of invective directed at "the big boys from outside who are coming in and spoiling it for us little guys," but you'll have to take that talk with a modest dose of skepticism since it is usually the influx of the "big boys" that increases land values in an area. If you are early enough in the market, they may also make your investment a better one.

The local board of realtors is an especially good source of current information about new laws and ordinances and ones that are proposed that could affect the value of an investment.

Time and time again we'll be coming back to the new ordinances and laws that may affect zoning and land use in general. We'll risk being repetitious because the political pressure being exerted at every level of government by the environmentalists is creating changes so quickly in primary people-pressure areas of the United States that one cannot be warned too often to keep up with them on a week-to-week basis.

In assessing the future value of any real estate investment, it is vital to know as much as possible about the local or regional *political climate*. There is a certain degree of in-built hazard in trying to think ahead of political events. Investors and speculators are born optimists. If the possibility of a fine profit motivates your search for an investment, then most assuredly you will be tempted to look with more interest at the rosy side of the picture. It is tough to be realistic. Sometimes events that one cannot possibly anticipate make the realistic appraisal of an investment situation all but impossible. But you'll have the odds going with you if you do all you can to inform yourself about the past, present and probable future of any investment area that interests you. The essential difference between the amateur and the professional lies in solid information properly equated and applied. *The only magic ingredient in good land investment is common sense.* And the soundest application of common sense is to ask *pertinent questions.* In each of the following chapters we have tried to emphasize the basic questions the buyer should ask the seller. *Unless these answers add up, the deal probably won't!*

Before we get to specific types of land investment, however, let's take a brief look at the philosophical change that is taking place in the traditional uses of our land. As you undoubtedly know, "philosophy is the science which investigates the facts and principles of reality, and of human nature and conduct."*

The new factors that affect land investment—the sudden and sometimes disruptive preoccupation with environmentalism, conservation and preservation—are the direct effect of causal abuses that long ago should have begun to alarm a great many of us. These new forces come into conflict with those who conceive their own economic advantage as lying in the status quo. It is another manifestation of the eternal battle—man in conflict with himself.

Let us see how one aspect of that conflict is presently affecting the American life-style.

---

*Webster's New Collegiate Dictionary.

5.
The Open-Space Age

Whenever private industry ignores an area of public responsibility, it risks government intervention and invites the establishment of still another bureaucracy.

Whenever government abdicates an area of public trust, it invites the intervention of militant citizen groups.

It was precisely this abdication of responsibility and breach of public trust on the part of both the developers and government, where land planning and development were concerned, that brought into being the militant environmentalists and activated the principle of the equal opposite force.

It's a shame that we must always wait until there have been flagrant abuses before we set in motion the forces necessary to guard against them. And it is too bad because one extreme begets another. Ideally, the solution would lie in a system of ongoing industry and government checks and balances. Perhaps that is where the present conflict between the exploiters, on the one hand, and the radical environmentalists, on the other, is taking us. In the process, however, a lot of innocent bystanders who based their security on long-term land investments are

getting hurt. Some of them are finding their life savings dissipated by continuing taxes and assessments on property that has been frozen as the result of hastily conceived emergency ordinances that purport to allow local, regional and federal bureaucracies sufficient time to study the situation.

Farmers and ranchers in areas coveted by unbridled "land butchers" and developers are being forced into bankruptcy or into unwanted sales because tax-hungry county officials have arbitrarily increased assessed valuation on entire areas. These officials based their blanket increases on the false "market value" of raw parcels whacked into rough, unimproved two and one-half acre *ranchitos* or *personal farms* that have been pressure-sold to foolish buyers for as much as ten times their actual value.

For the past ten years, well over a million acres a year have been so affected. In the South and West and Southwest, once great ranches have been parceled up and peddled to space-hungry, absentee urban owners who not only have *not seen* what they purchased from slick sales pitches, but probably never will. This is also true of Florida.

3. The magic link between progress and profit! The ultranew Antelope Valley Freeway connecting the Los Angeles megalopolis with the last large area in Southern California suitable for urban development.

Visible in the lower right-hand corner, two huge new shopping complexes. A new hospital can be seen in the upper right-hand corner and, in the upper center, another new shopping complex and a new residential development that, shortly, will fill the open, one-time alfalfa fields solidly with residences and commercial enterprises. Six years ago, this freeway was a dotted line marked "proposed" on most maps and was openly called "a real estate promoters' dream!" [Photograph courtesy of Stubbings Studio, Lancaster, California.]

And in this manner, for all intents and purposes, vast areas of America's precious open space have disappeared. Much of the land has been sold to foreign owners. Tens of thousands of Japanese, Chinese, West Germans and Filipinos have bought a little piece of America—*sight unseen*—from overseas salesmen. Hundreds of thousands of native-born Americans have done the same thing. Few will have made sound investments unless they have been fortunate enough to fall into the hands of an ethical professional developer who had fully disclosed all of the essential information and who had actually planned the development in a manner to insure controlled growth and improvement.

Some "paradise peddlers" with no concern for any values, least of all environmental values, have crisscrossed the country optioning vacant or open land with minimal front money, paying it off a piece at a time with "leverage dollars" (the "OPM Purchase Principle"—*O*ther *P*eople's *M*oney), recording sales totaling a half million dollars a month and more, stuffing their pockets with exorbitant profits and moving on to ravage a new area with their high-pressure razzle-dazzle.

Earlier we pointed out that we now have four times as many Americans per square mile of land than we had a century ago. That is true, but it does not mean that every square mile of land in our country has become four times more valuable as a result.

The land that has become more valuable—some of it *four thousand* times more valuable—is land that lay, or presently lies, in areas of increasing people pressure, and land peripheral to such areas. The very remote desert and hill country wilderness that we dubbed "West Hellangone" in *The Simple Truth about Western Land Investment,* in most cases has little foreseeable future as a sound investment in this century. Certainly, in a special situation, a sound investment may be found in such land today. But with the United States suddenly aware of its rapidly disappearing open space, even land of potential future value may be tied up indefinitely by new ordinances, laws and environmental impact studies.

A realistic investor today will take into most serious account the new mood in America. In Paris, in 1936, *Le Paris Soir* feature editor, Gilbert Stieble, asked us if it was still true that in the United States "there is more space where nobody is than where anybody is."

When we answered, "Probably so," he gazed at the crowd streaming down the Champs Elysées and eddying around our sidewalk table at Fouquet's. "It is true," he said. "And that is what makes your America great!"

Gilbert is gone now, shot down in flames over North Africa by three Nazi fighter pilots who jumped him out of the sun. Suffer though he must have, we believe this incredible French-Canadian journalist, fighter-adventurer who so loved open space, would have suffered more had he lived to see high rises in Paris and rampant urban and suburban sprawl everywhere.

It may be technically true that there is still more space where nobody is than where anybody is. But to one who has roamed this country from border to border and coast to coast, who has revisited once remote wilderness areas, who has climbed most of our challenging mountains only to find the thoughtless litter of a horde of predecessors, it would seem more likely that now, with All Terrain Vehicles, and motorcycles and those "Abominable Snow Machines," someone is everywhere all of the time. And this new mobility is what the exploiters of our remaining remote open land count on. It is also what motivates the passionate opposition of those who would conserve our diminishing open space.

The "Open-Space Syndrome," beginning as it did with the preservation of public land in state and national parks and forest preserves, has spread to the cities now, where streets have become glass-walled canyons whose sides are higher than their blocks are long.

And it has spread to suburbs where town commons, village greens and squares have been destroyed by short-sighted developers with an insatiable hunger for close-in real estate.

A recent headline in a building trades magazine read, "Con-servationists—Saviors or Saboteurs?" We expected a severely prejudiced story and were surprised to find instead a rational analysis of the new situation confronting the developers and builders. The thrust of the article was that many, if not most, developers were "too close to their houses to see the towns they were creating."

"We have asked for this environmentalist opposition," the article said, "by emphasizing what has been 'good business' for us in the short term; and in so doing have created long-term problems that could destroy us. Maximum density may never have been good business. Certainly it isn't now. The cry for innovative land use and more open space is unmistakable; and the developer who persists in influencing local authorities to grant variances for high densities is presiding at his own funeral."

As true as that is, many a developer, driven by rising land and material costs and constantly escalating labor charges, is still trying to squeeze out the maximum number of sites per acre. It is this group that sees the conservationist and environmentalist as saboteurs—"nature nuts who are more concerned with animal habitats than with human housing."

But the realists among the land developers recognize that these groups are with us now, a permanent part of the national scene, and that they are winning public and political support.

Under pressure from the environmentalists, land planners and architects are becoming innovators. On their drafting boards are challenging new concepts that range from "vertical density" planning to conserve limited urban open space to "satellite villages" linked to metropolitan centers in a way that will change the style of suburban life and alter the anatomy of the conventional megalopolis.

A stimulating example of the new direction in total com-munity planning has been seen by hundreds of thousands of visitors to General Electric's free exhibit* at California's Disney-

---

*First exhibited at the World's Fair, New York City, 1965.

land. These visitors look with admiration and envy, aware that only on the drafting board can a city start from scratch. So they leave the exciting exhibit a bit wistfully, knowing that if such a transformation is ever to take place in their communities, it will require generations. But these new concepts are taking hold. Change has become inevitable and the practical-minded land investor will watch carefully the new directions, and seek a place in the new order that will fit his purse and fulfill its promise of profit.

Bless them or damn them—the environmentalists, the ecologists, the conservationists, the preservationists—all are with us for keeps. Certain that their cause is righteous and sure of public support, a score of dedicated groups will continue to plead, to prod and to pressure in their efforts to save us from suffocating in our own polluted air, from poisoning ourselves with our own polluted water and from imprisoning ourselves in parcels of land designed more to profit the promoter than please the people.

The conservationists are the "equal opposite force" in the ecology equation. Their counter power has been generated by the mindless abuses of the past. They have been called "over-zealous," "unrealistic," and occasionally "superficial" in their concerns. But the sum total of their anxiety over the physical state of our union can only result in an increase in the worth of those natural resources that come under realistic new planning.

Whether or not one agrees with their methods, even the most prejudiced will have to concede that many urgent reforms would not have been initiated had the conservationists not sounded their warnings and mustered their forces for political action.

In general the most seriously affected industries no longer oppose them in principle. They are beginning to cooperate; but as the spokesman for one nationwide development corporation put it:

"Certainly good ecology is good business. But we are operating under zoning that was approved by responsible county and state authorities at the time we began our land use engineering. Where programs have been set in motion and where sales schedules have been initiated on earlier profit projections we just can't turn around overnight. We need time to balance out our commitments. We are now in the position of having to fight for time or go down the tube."

Most alarming to these men were Senate Bill 632 and House Bill 7211, both apparently now dead but certain to be revived in some compromised form in the 1973 congressional session. Opponents of the Senate Bill were particularly alarmed by the provision that granted federal aid to those states which brought their land use legislation into conformity with the federal law—but applied frightening political pressure on those who might resist, by withholding federal funds for highway, airport and urban renewal.

"It is legal blackmail," complained one large developer. "The damned bills will make it impossible to get any decisions. We'll have still another layer of government bureaucracy to deal with. The home building industry is second only to the food industry. If they hobble us, the whole economy is apt to fall apart. We need balance. The conservationist lobbies are panicking the politicians into acting too quickly. So we've got to lobby too."

The process is similar to those kinetic toys we used to see—the groups of suspended steel balls that were set banging against each other. Moving in diminishing arcs, they finally settled down. And so will the opposing forces in the land development and land conservation ranks.

Our primary resource is our land. Simplistic though it may sound, it is nonetheless true that when these opposing forces finally balance out, well-located, well-planned real estate will prove to be an even better investment than it has been in the past.

We will have pleasant communities in which to live. We will have green belts and open space in the form of city, county and state parks. We'll have more national parks also. *And we will have to pay for them.*

One thing that is worrisome about the militant idealists among the conservationists is their apparent total unconcern with how the land is to be paid for. New land, acquired from private owners, will have to be bought at fair market value. That means it will come off the tax rolls. And the effect of that will be to reduce tax income at all levels, at a time when all levels of government are growing more and more expensive.

The inevitable effect will be an increase in the assessed valuation of private property that lies within the tax influence region of the new public land. So we must be prepared for higher taxes on our homes and businesses unless—miracle of miracles—government at all levels is finally driven to sufficient economies in operation to absorb the difference. Even *The Man of La Mancha* would hardly dare entertain that "impossible dream"!

6.
The Land Market

In 1964, when *The Simple Truth about Western Land Investment* was first published, we listed five basic types of investment land. They were the following:

Urban land
Suburban land
Farm land
Recreation land
Raw land

It should be obvious that under each heading there are various choices. Land becomes a generic term for a commodity. Just as apples, oranges, lemons and bananas are all fruit but each differs from the other, so the various types of real estate are all land; but, most assuredly, they all differ.

At the time that first book appeared, the emphasis was on raw land investment, much of which turned out to have been the rankest sort of speculation. In fact, it was our awareness of the abuses in this field that prompted us to write a book that would give the buyer enough basic information to enable him to defend himself against high pressure land salesmen. Incidentally, they are still with us, using somewhat more sophisticated techniques now. In the chapter "The High-Pressure Pitch," we will describe them and give you an inside glimpse of how they work to rack up more than $800 million in land sales each year despite growing legal restrictions.

Each of the five basic forms of land investment continues to offer its unique advantages. However, in the past several years the emphasis has switched from raw land to developed recreational and second-home land. Under the second category we would also have to include farm land, particularly in New England which, much to the consternation of many natives, has been "discovered" by the urbanites from New York and Boston. In subsequent chapters where we examine investment options in some detail, we'll talk about some of the repercussions being caused by these "weekend farmers."

Urban Land

As for urban land, except for a personal homesite, it has seldom been a practical investment for the average "individual" buyer since, by the time an area is urbanized, real estate values have escalated beyond his reach. There are exceptions, of course. A good residential lot—a "fixer-upper" residence—or small commercial structure may come on the market and be within the means of a small investor, preferably a buyer, with the energy and know-how to enhance its value by remodeling for a capital gains resale.

In general, however, in the larger cities, urban land and the financing of it have become so sophisticated that only professional realtors, builders and lending institutions can handle it successfully. It is beyond the purview of this book, which is really a "primer" on land investment for the average American, to get into the Coldwell-Banker—Douglas Elliman league. That, indeed, is another "ball game."

Suburban Land

Suburban real estate offers a little more possibility for modest investment, particularly in those new suburbs which are still desirable in the sense that they are modern and growing.

In such an area the prospective investor would expect to find a "sellers' market," a market where "buyer demand" works in favor of the seller—supply and demand again. But there are always "good buys"—bona fide bargains—even in a general sellers' market area. So we would not rule out some suburbs as areas of possible fine real estate investments.

In mid-1972 the building industry estimated that the residential market would be approximately 2 million units a year for the next three years. The preponderance of that construction will take place on large parcels of preplanned land purchased by developers with national and international operations. Again, it is not a game where the "little guy" can usually sit in. Still, many small, well-informed investors have made sizable fortunes by studying expansion patterns—analyzing people-pressure points correctly—and taking predevelopment positions in fairly substantial parcels of land which later have been sold in one transaction to an incoming home builder who is "putting his tract together."*

More often than not the small investor in suburban land will do better to buy early in a good subdivision and "ride up with the rising values." But there is no infallible formula for doing that either. A lot of factors must be taken into account when a family buys a home. For want of some *simple but sound*

---

*Acquiring the bulk acreage needed for his subdivision.

research, a family may find it necessary, along with many of their neighbors, to plant a For Sale sign on the lawn and pray that they can get out even. In its proper place, we'll suggest how a prospective suburban buyer may do much to insure making a wise investment.

Recreational Land

Investments in recreational property require a whole new set of criteria. In this era of more leisure, of greater mobility over roads and airways that reduce grandfather's "long day's journey" to a matter of minutes, we Americans are suddenly confronted with a bewildering number of choices.

Do we ski? Do we fish? Do we camp? Do we golf? Do we swim? Do we ride? Do we bicycle? Do we enjoy a combination of these activities? And do we manage our varied recreational activities on a year-around basis in one place, or in several?

Read the advertisements, or look and listen to them on TV and radio, and you will see that we are tempted with a veritable "plethora of pleasures."

No people in the entire recorded history of mankind has ever been confronted with so many options. We are faced with myriad temptations to invest. As a result, even the most cautious buyers stand in real danger of acting on impulse, without taking that "second look around" that is so essential to a sound "dollar judgment." In no other investment does a salesman have such a strong emotional "hook" on the family as a whole.

Recreational properties are the "hot items" in the land market now. And the situation is likely to persist for some time to come. We intend no pun when we say that it is easy to get caught up in the "ground swell" of publicity. But we certainly intend a word of caution when we say that many of the outright or implied promises made by enthusiastic salesman need careful examination. One of the easiest places to get in over your head is in recreational land investment. In subsequent chapters we'll examine the pros and cons of this sort of investment in some detail also.

Raw Land

Raw land may have been displaced as the "hot item" in real estate promotion now. But the clever salesman can still sink a sharp hook into his prospect, particularly if the family is one that wants to get away from the crowd, or if the buyer just wishes to satisfy his atavistic compulsion to own a piece of the good earth for himself for whatever rationalization he may devise.

The skilled buyer of raw land, as we point out in *The Simple Truth* book, is aiming to make a long-term investment on his path of progress. The procedure here is to research various areas of potential people pressure, buy in early and hold for a reasonable time. The end objective is a capital gain.

Thousands of persons have been persuaded to do that—too many of them in the wrong places. We call those remote "unanchored" areas "West Hellangone." But raw land, purchased in well-researched areas for realistic prices, can be one of the most rewarding and least troublesome investments a person can make. More about that later too—in detail!

Whom to buy from? Any owner with a piece of real estate that has increased in value is a potential seller. A knowledgeable investor who knows what he's doing, who knows what questions to ask, may often save thousands of dollars in commissions by purchasing directly from the seller. But those buyers are a very small minority. As a rule the prospective land investor will do far better to deal with a reputable professional—a licensed broker. Most of them will display a Realtor's seal. Otherwise, deal with a consultant and appraiser who is also a Realtor.

The trademark REALTOR indicates a broker who has been accepted into membership in his local real estate board and the National Association of Real Estate Boards and is pledged to its established code of business ethics.

We would have to say that human nature being what it is, the *Realtor* seal in the window, and on the business cards and stationery, is no absolute guarantee that a few mavericks won't be tempted to stretch the truth a bit. (After all, a few cross-bearing ministers have been known to break a Commandment or two!) But, generally speaking, the Realtor takes his obligation under the code seriously. The great bulk of real estate transactions in this country will be handled through the offices of the 100,000 brokers who display the seal.

This is not to infer that many brokers who, for one reason or another, have *not* joined the national organization are not entirely reputable men and women. If a customer has any doubt, it is simple enough to check a broker's reputation in an area by asking around. Banks, savings and loan companies, title companies—the people a broker must do business with—will know.

If the broker's reputation is good, they will be happy to say so. If it is not, you may draw your own conclusions from their reticence or refusal to answer your queries. But for heaven's sake, use a little subtlety in your questioning. Don't walk up to a bank vice-president and abruptly ask, "Is broker Jones an honest man?" If you are going to deal with a broker, quite probably you will also be dealing with a lending institution and a title company. Tell them you are thinking about making a purchase. Mention the names of the brokers to whom you have been talking. In the ensuing easy, general conversation, you'll find out all you need to know about the broker *and* the banker.

A broker may not necessarily know all that you will need to know about a special piece of real estate. We have met many reputable brokers who have become so involved in some narrow aspect of their area that they have not had the time or the need to inform themselves in depth about values of certain other types of real estate investment. In such a case, it may be wise to enlist the services of a qualified appraiser.

How do you determine such a person's qualifications? An effective appraiser should have a thorough knowledge of all phases of real estate and be a licensed broker. He should be familiar with real estate tax studies, highest and best use studies, feasibility studies for property development, real estate valuations for both buyer and seller interests and market surveys. And today, an appraiser should know about new ecological laws that can affect the land that interests you. Question the person on the breadth of his knowledge.

A good appraisal report (whether you hire a professional or do your own research) should contain photographs of the property, a site diagram with a complete legal description and a map showing the exact location. And most important—a value estimate, preferably with a map showing location of comparable sales. Also, weather conditions, recreational facilities or opportunities, living amenities, utilities and the area's tax structure should be included in the report.

Because of the "new look" in land investment, you may very well be doing business with the developer himself and his "in-house" sales department or the sales organization he has contracted with to represent his properties.

Here again you'll be dealing with licensed real estate salesmen and with their broker or brokers. In most states, there must be a broker between the buyer and the seller if a licensed salesman is involved in the transaction. A real estate salesman may not enter the transaction without a broker. Why? Because the buying and selling of real estate can be a complicated process, indeed, a skilled profession. As in any profession, its practitioners must be trained.

A salesperson has studied hard to learn the rudiments of the profession. The license is evidence that the basic requirements have been met. The next step is to study for a broker's license.

To use an analogy, the person must serve an internship—as a doctor must—before hanging out a shingle. So salespeople must sell through a broker, but a broker may act alone.

In the first case, the broker is your "backup" guarantee that the details of the purchase will be in order. The commission the seller pays (the scales vary with the type and amount of the transaction) may be considered as a one-shot insurance premium—"A damn-foolishness indemnity," one seller calls it.

A great many real estate brokers around the country, wishing to expand their prospect lists, have joined one of several huge franchise real estate firms.

Most of us have seen signs reading Strout Realty and United Farm Agency, among others. These are national organizations that have put together a sort of super-sales cooperative with hundreds of small brokers in every part of the nation. In return for the national catalogue listings the member brokers receive on properties in their area, they share their commissions with the central organization.

If you have ever thumbed through a United Farm Agency catalogue, it will be immediately apparent that a family wishing to invest in some distant area that interests them, can get a fine preliminary idea of a piece of property from the photographs and from the local broker's data that are included in the captions. In the case of the UFA, most of the listings will be on rural properties as opposed to urban and suburban offerings, which explains why this type of franchise broker is popular with buyers looking for rural retreats, small "gentlemen's farms" and future retirement places.

In the end, of course, the transaction gets down to the local broker and all of the same precautionary rules must apply.

Most of the new suburban residential and recreational-cum-second-home developments are now being done by huge corporations. Many of them are conglomerates with little or no prior history in real estate sales. But they bring to land development their access to vast capital resources, the money to buy "the best management, planning and sales brains" in the industry and

4. *Two approaches to land use at Incline Village, Lake Tahoe, Nevada. To many planners, the high rise (left) makes much more esthetic and economic sense than the row structures since it occupies less impervious ground space and houses more families "under one roof" than the spread-out multiple condominiums. Incidentally, the mottled surface of the water is not man-made "pollution" but an annual phenomenon at most High Sierra lakes—a dusting of pollen from the evergreens. It soon disappears. [Photograph courtesy of Chapman Wentworth, Wentworth & Associates.]*

the financing needed for high pressure merchandising. Later in this book there is much more detail presented about the way these huge operations go about getting our attention, and often our interest.

There is one more aspect of the land market that should be included here. It is not strictly a *direct investment* in real estate since it involves pooling your money with others to buy shares in an investment trust.

The operation is called an REIT—an abbreviation for Real Estate Investment Trust. This, too, we will examine later in detail since it is one of the few opportunities available to the small investor who wishes to sit in a "big game" with a minimum of risk.

To sum up: We have seen that there are several *basic options* open to the modest investor in the land market, plus the REIT. And we have seen that land is sold directly by the owner, or through a broker via the salesperson, or by the broker alone, dealing directly with the customer on behalf of the seller.

We have said that today, because of new ecological considerations and political pressure from conservationist groups, investing in land is somewhat more complicated than it used to be. For those who do not inform themselves—and who do not make certain of the people they are dealing with—land investment can indeed be more hazardous. But that would apply to any investment if one is uninformed.

We believe—and have demonstrated it in our personal land investment program—that these new considerations can actually enhance the possibility of dealing profitably.

7.
Land Language

As with any marketable commodity, land must be "packaged" in uniform recognizable quantities. Like many commodities, land may be sold in bulk or it may be parceled into smaller units. The smallest of these units would be the average city lot. The largest would be the giant ranches that often include within their boundaries hundreds of *square miles* of range and crop land.

The *square mile* may be said to be the basic land unit. It is called a *section* of land. It contains 640 *acres*.

NOTE: ALL SECTION BOUNDARIES RUN NORTH AND SOUTH, AND EAST AND WEST.

Sections of land are divided into quarters by median lines that run north and south and east and west. Each of these *quarter sections* contains 160 acres (640 acres divided by 4).

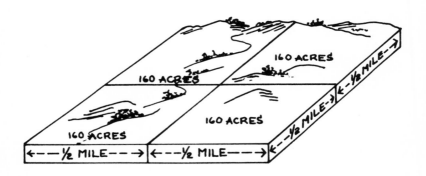

TOTAL = 640 ACRES OR 1 SECTION.

In turn, each of these quarter sections is divided into quarters containing 40 acres each (160 acres divided by 4).

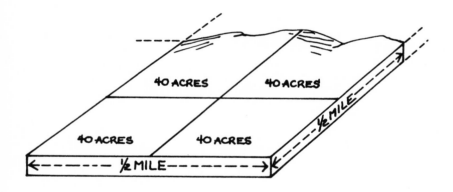

TOTAL = 160 ACRES, 1/4 SECTION.

In the Iowa corn belt it is not uncommon to hear a working farmer with a quarter of a section of land say, "Let's start pickin' in the southwest 'forty'."

From the illustration below, we can easily see how he has located the area he wants to start harvesting in.

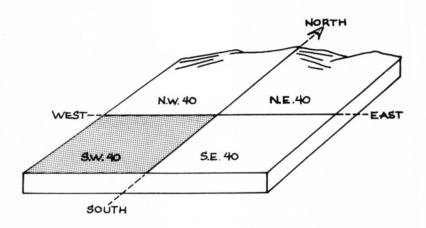

This illustrates the principle behind the subdivision and location of all basic parcels of land. When we get down to the incorporated city lot the procedure changes a bit. Then Tract numbers and Lot numbers are used to find and legally describe these small individual parcels of land. But for now, let us stay with basic subdivision procedures.

Now it must be obvious that land does not always have to be divided into four parts. Suppose a farmer only wanted to buy a half section—320 acres. The section could be divided into halves in two ways:

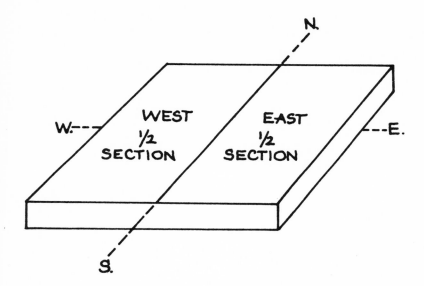

OR IT CAN BE DIVIDED THIS WAY:

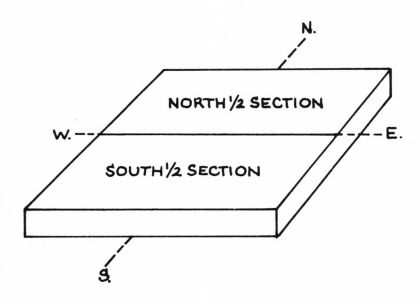

In turn, these half sections (320 acres) can be divided in two ways:

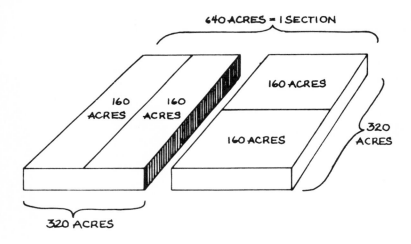

Now that the logic and the procedure of this system are clear, let's do an illustration that breaks this method down to its smallest practical unit—the 2½-acre parcel:

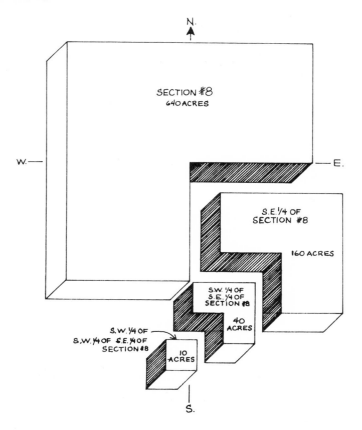

640 acres = 1 mile x 1 mile
320 acres = 1 mile x 1/2 mile
160 acres = 1/2 mile x 1/2 mile
 80 acres = 1/2 mile x 1/4 mile
 40 acres = 1/4 mile x 1/4 mile
 20 acres = 1/4 mile x 1/8 mile
 10 acres = 1/8 mile x 1/8 mile
  5 acres = 660 feet x 330 feet
 2½ acres = 330 feet x 330 feet
  1 acre = 4,840 square yards or
            43,560 square feet

Although it is not always done this way, a 2½-acre parcel may be subdivided into 10 one-quarter acre (gross) city lots as shown below. Streets, sidewalks, alleys and easements must be subtracted from the gross size.

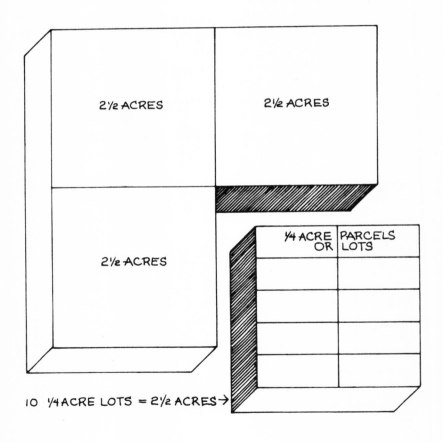

10 ¼ ACRE LOTS = 2½ ACRES →

Now suppose a salesman wants to show you a ten-acre parcel of land and you notice in his notes that it bears the legal description, "The southwest one-quarter of the southwest one-quarter of the southeast one-quarter of . . ." let's say Section 8. Don't grab your checkbook and run. He is not trying to double-talk you. What seems to be a masterpiece of real estate obfuscation is really a simple and logical procedure for locating your land exactly.

If you can remember that all section lines run due *north* and *south* and due *east* and *west,* it becomes clear that when a square mile of land is divided into quarters, and those quarters are also divided into quarters, and those quarters are again divided into quarters, their boundary lines still run north and south and east and west. What you have is quarters within quarters within quarters, somewhat like those wonderful Chinese lacquer boxes that fit neatly into one another.

If you approach this next illustration with a feeling of curiosity and discovery, the alleged mystery of legal land description will clear up in thirty seconds—particularly if you envision the whole thing as simply being a matter of *squares within squares.* (See illustration on following page.)

We have talked about the basic land measurement unit, the section. But that also lies in another larger unit called a township. So your piece of property which we have located from its legal description as the southwest quarter of the southwest quarter of the southeast quarter of Section 8 needs still another "umbrella designation" to isolate it from all its neighbors.

For convenience's sake, surveyors created the township unit, a block of 36 sections. Since we now know that a section is one square mile, it follows that 36 sections would make a township equal to 36 square miles. Obviously, the number of townships in a state will depend upon the size of the state. For the sake of illustration we are going to create a state, a square one, somewhat resembling New Mexico or Colorado or Wyoming if their edges were to be "tidied up."

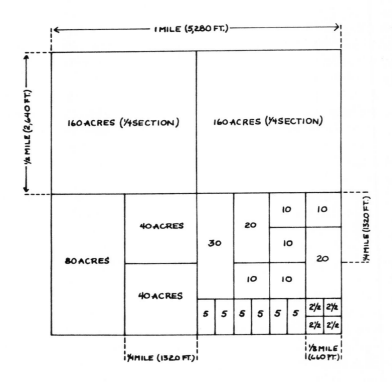

SOUTHWEST QUARTER OF THE SOUTHWEST QUARTER OF THE SOUTH-
EAST QUARTER OF SECTION 8.

As we did in our first land book, we'll call the state West Utopia. (Others may call it North, East or South Utopia if they wish. "West" implies no prejudice on the authors' part. The most successful land investment we ever made was in the east, in Suffolk County, New York.)

Arbitrarily we'll say our state contains 100 townships. Now look at illustration #9 and you'll see that these townships are also divided by a north-south line and an east-west line. Again, this quartering process gives us some lines of reference from which we can start to locate the section in which your land lies.

The north-south line is called the Meridian Line. The east-west line is called the Base Line. Townships in our state are said to be located *north* or *south* of the Base Line and *east* or *west* of the Meridian Line.

The strips of townships running from east to west are called Tiers. The strips of townships running north and south are called Ranges.

So now, by examining our fictitious state we will discover that each of the 100 townships it contains can be located through this relationship to a base and meridian line.

Let's say that at the end of the legal description of your ten-acre parcel we see the legend, "T-3-N, R-4-W." Translated to "land language" that means, "Tier 3 North, Range 4 West."

Now look at the map of our state-of-convenience, and you will see how our township was picked out from the other 99.

Remember now that what we are looking at is a *township.* That little township square contains 36 sections, each one mile square. Your land is located in one of those sections. It is not important for our purposes to go into more graphs to show you how sections are numbered within a township. Now the full legal description of your ten acres would read: "The southwest quarter of the southwest quarter of the southeast quarter of Section 8, Township (Tier) 3 North, Range 4 West—or T-3-N, R-4-W." And then we'd add the county name—Kern, for instance, and the state. In actual practice there would be another

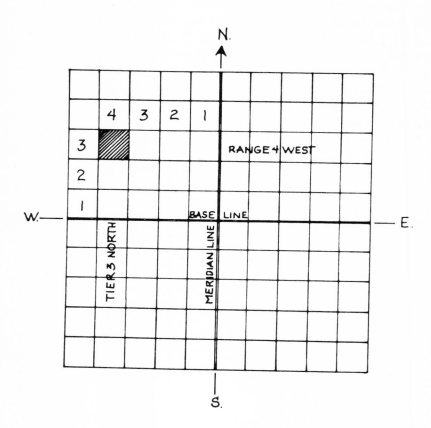

symbol—something like SBBM. In California that means San Bernardino Base Meridian to differentiate the particular part of the state in which our block of townships is located. A state with only 100 townships would be a tiny state indeed. But small or large, it is necessary to break up states into a number of different base meridian sectors. The county name helps to locate the general area.

So there it is, the mystery debunked. It is simple geometry—the business of making squares (sometimes rectangles and occasionally triangles) within squares until you have squeezed down the boundaries to your particular piece of real estate.

A little practice with some scratch paper and an outline of a hypothetical section will make you as expert as the broker whose "cryptography," until now, has seemed like a cross between runic writing and Sanskrit. You'll find it is fun, too. And chances are you'll get some admiring "oohs" and "ahhhs" from your less "learned" friends.

If you now have a clear picture of how land is "packaged" for sale, we'll move on to the heart of the matter—the technique of choosing the best land investment for your needs.

8.
The Second-Home Boom

It is probably no exaggeration to say that the recreational second-home boom is as solid as the desires of approximately 170 million persons (who live in sixty-six urban centers of a half million population and over) to escape from the city for part of each year.

According to the National Association of Home Builders, around two and a half million families presently own second homes. They estimate, conservatively, that 100,000 new recreational second homes are being built each year.

The American Land Development Association, a newly organized group of subdividers, is more optimistic. It estimates that second homes may proliferate by as much as 200,000 a year. Almost everyone who has looked into the matter estimates that by 1980 Americans seeking relief from the compression and pollution of the big cities and their suburbs will have bought upward of 5 million such homes. The United States Office of Interstate Land Sales states that transactions for second homes are running at an average of $5 billion a year.

In its revised figures, worked up from the 1970 tally, the Bureau of the Census found out that urban population in the United States is up only 1 percent over the 1960 figure. But suburban population is up over 28 percent. By 1980 the bureau predicts that one-half of our population will be living in the suburbs and only one-quarter will remain in the urban centers. The remainder will be trying to fight off the invasion of "city dwellers" who are fed up and want to come share the blessings of open space and clean air still to be found in the rural areas. "And these city people," warn the conservationists, "will move out across the open land bringing their own cloud of pollution with them!"

The effect of this people pressure has been to increase by 20 percent the price of desirable land in the country within a two- to three-hour throughway drive. The increases have taken place within the past five years. In the most desirable areas it is not uncommon to find that land prices have increased 300 percent in the same period. In the chapter, "The New Country 'Gentle-people'," we will quote from letters received in response to queries from family and close friends who have opted for what columnist Max Lerner calls, ". . . this kind of alternating bipolar life."

Not all of these people have chosen small weekend farms or *ranchitos.* Many of them have bought into the huge new second-home developments that are scattered across the length and breadth of our land and onto its island states, territorial holdings and protectorates.

Many of the new owners are disillusioned summer and winter vacationers who crowded into our thirty-five national parks only to find conditions worse than those from which they were seeking relief. Since 1940 we have nearly doubled our population; but in that same time span we have created only six new national parks, one of which (Guadalupe Mountains, Texas) has not been open to the public.

Responding to the pressure of these millions of people who feel they must have at least temporary annual relief from their urban existence, developers have begun to create planned recreational communities that, in effect, are miniparks. Some of these offer outright ownership of land parcels, complete with an array of "club facilities." Others offer condominium living with complete all-year recreation facilities and an undivided interest in the open space that, thanks to the conservationists, has recently become the developers' most attractive sales angle.

While looking into huge new planned recreational communities being constructed around Phoenix, Arizona, we visited Frank Lloyd Wright's "Taliesin," a home so ingeniously designed of native materials and so well integrated into its surroundings that it is all but invisible until one is less than a quarter of a mile from it.

There we learned that as early as 1930 the great architect had predicted our return to rural life, envisioning Americans working in cities only three days a week and spending the other four on their own "green acre" under conditions more natural to man. The "out-migration" happened somewhat sooner than the genius designer had predicted, primarily because we urban animals were a great deal slower than he presumed we would be in altering our big city life-style to more pleasant patterns. It will be another half century before we finally get around to redesigning our great urban centers to accomplish that. In the meantime, we will need the best of these second-home retreats. Because greed plus need can make us myopic to the point of blindness, many hastily conceived so-called second-home recreational developments will be pressure-sold to the unwary that, in time, may become unanchored rural slums. That, too, is what the conservationists are trying to prevent through the adoption of commonsense planning restraints.

Earlier we spoke of the "equal opposite force" that these ecology and conservation groups represent, and we observed that, in our opinion, the net of their long-term opposition will enhance land values. Perhaps we should add here that as taxpayers all of us are involved in the land business. If the conservationists, applying their political pressure, manage to stall the development of great amounts of recreational land and finally move Congress into appropriating public money to buy it, we shall have to pay for it. And that will be done through *added taxes* on the developed property we already own and through the general fund. There is sure to be a collision between rank emotionalism and economic realism. As taxpaying voters it behooves all of us who have, or yearn to have, a second-home recreational place to watch very carefully the legislation that Congress will be asked to create and pass. If millions of acres of privately owned open land are taken into the public domain, sooner or later they will have to be paid for at fair market value. Even if such acreage is presently taxed as range land or timberland, it will mean millions of dollars removed from the property tax rolls; and more tens of millions will have to be produced by new taxation to make up for the loss and provide more funds for the acquisition of still more privately held land.

We need to act thoughtfully in the rush to save open land, and we need more second-home subdividers and recreational developers who will act with unusual foresight and uncharacteristic unselfishness. This is necessary if we are to prevent the loading of our courts with suits filed by owners seeking relief from what, in effect, amounts to inverse condemnation—a disastrous breach of the rights of individual ownership.

What alarms the conservationists, in addition to the wanton cutting of prime timber to meet our housing boom and to satisfy the overseas market (primarily in Japan), is the fact that more than one million acres of prime recreational land are disappearing each year. Most of it is being bought up by huge corporations which are rushing to get their share of the growing market for second-home recreational real estate.

Many of the most thoughtful developers, usually those who have been in the industry for a generation or more, foresee and fear as inevitable a federal land use law. They are realists. They know that no omnibus law can equitably cover all areas. They know that such a law will stop everything cold until it can be shaken down, probably through drawn-out court procedures, and be made to work justly for all. They know that before that happens the new bureaucracy in Washington will have to hand back to the states and counties much of the responsibility of interpreting and administering the law at those levels. And they know that local conservationist groups will undoubtedly challenge any decisions in favor of development, thereby creating still more people pressure in a second-home market unable to meet the demand.

What does this have to do with the value of second-home recreational land as an investment? It means that those developments that meet the criteria outlined in the following chapter *could prove* to be excellent investments indeed. Nobody can predict for certain, but in the next few pages you'll find out what you can do to make as good a judgment as anybody *if* you'll just take the same amount of time and interest you probably devote to handicapping a horse, a football team, a baseball team or whatever sport "turns you on."

Limited private recreational space will mean a "seller's market." *It is in this atmosphere that pressure sales techniques can move a customer to make irrational judgments.*

"Caveat emptor" read the Latin sign on some of Rome's most dubious "merchandise." *Let the buyer beware*—as sound advice now as then!

9.
Recreational and/or Second-Home Land

There is no such thing as a "bad land investment" if you are genuinely happy with it. *A substantial portion of the profit in any such investment should be reckoned in pleasure received.* Often this is not the case because shortly after the commitment is made a reaction called "buyer's remorse" sets in. That is particularly true if one has been subjected to the process that real estate "pitchmen" call "the pressure cooker." Even a Howard Hughes can find himself paying through both ends of the purse.

A land investment—any sort of land investment—is likely to involve a major commitment on the part of the purchaser. So it's only human to have second thoughts about it. As long as we have been investing in land we still have an occasional twinge of buyer's remorse—a moment of wondering whether, in our enthusiasm, we have overlooked some critical element that might spell the difference between a poor choice and a good one.

Because of this, we seldom move hastily. And still, a time or two, we have made what could appear to others to be an impetuous decision. Recently we made such a move at Sunriver, Oregon, a remarkable recreational/second-home development that we'll discuss in detail within the next few pages. Sure enough, down the highway a few miles, we found ourselves asking each other if, in fact, we had refuted the practice we preach to others. After reviewing both our own needs and the fine print in the purchase agreement, we decided that we had acted prudently. We had asked all of the essential questions and had received plausible and quite probably truthful answers. Part of the stock-in-trade of a successful land sales person is a missionary's conviction and zeal. In the hands of a skilled salesperson, it is difficult indeed to keep from being "converted."

In the chapter, "The Land Market," we listed the five basic types of investment land as we saw them back in 1964 when we published our first "primer" on land investment. In the intervening years the emphasis has changed from raw land to recreational/second-home land. So we will discuss first the needs, real or imagined, that motivate you to start looking and some methods you can employ to find a promising area. Then we'll list some things you must find out in order to make certain it is the right area for you; and, finally, some questions you must ask to make reasonably certain you will be making a wise investment with a real potential for both pleasure and profit.

Some of the following is going to seem unnecessarily obvious. And still it is a verified fact that thousands of men and women make choices without ever having really considered some of the most basic questions pertaining to their wants and needs. For instance, here is an excerpt from a letter received in September of 1968—one of several hundred letters that are similar in tone:

> . . . We bought the condominium at_____ Mountain
> because both my husband and I thought we would
> enjoy the winter sports. It would be a new adventure
> for us. We were told that we could use the place for

several weeks in the winter, then rent it during the balance of the ski season for enough money to carry payments, maintenance, insurance—almost everything. And of course, we intended to use it during the summer also.

As it turned out, neither of us enjoyed skiing that much. We started too late in life, I guess! And we certainly didn't like the crowds on weekends and holidays. We couldn't even get to the store. More than that, the cold got to us. Certainly the place is wonderful for younger people who are really hooked on sliding down mountains. But for us—well, now we *know* we want something less active and more comfortable. Another trouble—the rentals did not come through. So many new places are being built for that market. And costs were much more than we estimated. We've been promised that we can get our money out, but so far the broker has not found a buyer. Meanwhile, the payments go on.

What we want now is a place in a milder climate— probably on a lake where we can have an inexpensive little boat and do some quiet fishing. But that will have to wait until we sell.

What we should have done was follow your advice and try renting for a season first. In the end we would have saved a small fortune in down payments, closing costs, maintenance, commissions, taxes, etc., not to mention about a thousand dollars worth of ski equipment that is now "out of style" and therefore unsalable. If we had read your book *before* and not *after* we could have saved thousands—a fact we freely confess.

The moral of this, and hundreds of other such stories that we have heard, is clear: Make certain you *know* what you really want in a recreational/second-home property before you commit yourself. Or as Samuel Johnson counseled back in the 1600s—

> . . . look before you ere you leap;
> For as you sow, ye are like to reap!

Caught in the crush and turmoil of a large city, you may long for the sylvan silence of the Maine woods or the solitude of a farm in New England's lovely mountain country. We could fill pages with the documented disillusionment of friends and strangers who have "dumped" on us, as our young people say in their pungent jargon.

How best to make certain? Budget a little time and money to "test hop" your "deep dream of peace." Spend all or part of your summer vacation in one of the locations that appeals to you. And if your plans include the possibility of one day turning a second home into a retirement place, then be certain you schedule a vacation in mid-winter also. Spring and autumn are usually deeply satisfying seasons anywhere—nature's times of future promise and past reflection. But what about mid-winter? Except for several especially favored areas—Hawaii, parts of Florida, parts of Arizona and Southern California—midwinter can be another matter! And even favored areas are known to suffer "unusual weather."

If you belong to the "get away from it all" school, it is not likely that you are going to be happy with an investment in a conventional recreational/second-home area. The basic economic requisites of such a development make mandatory a location that is readily accessible; and in time that spells the end of solitude. If you enjoy people (and most of us do) and if the development has been thoughtfully planned to provide community open space and relative privacy for homesites, then you may well find both sufficient solitude and the convenience and security of a good community— things most of us want.

The city dweller who longs to become a rural recluse will find the arguments, pro and con, in Chapter 12. (Parenthetically, we might get a bit ahead of ourselves and observe that this is an area of investment that is fraught with potential disaster, not the least of which is the possibility of being overrun by "civilization" anyway.)

Now then, what should you look for in a recreational/second-home investment? Where should you look? What questions should you ask?

We said earlier that, in making an investment such as this, it is wise to count part of your profit in pleasure derived. It would seem self-defeating to buy a place simply because it is a good investment dollar-wise. Usually, when dollars are unwisely spent, there is a chance to recover them or to earn more. When *years* are spent, they're spent, period. So reckon the amount of pleasure dividends you are going to receive from your investment. If you thoroughly enjoy the time spent at your vacation place, you are still ahead of the game—even if the real property value has not increased, which is highly unlikely if you have chosen well.

There are a lot of so-called recreational developments being advertised that are little more than raw land "mirage cities." In the section dealing with "land butchers," we'll examine a typical one. Many of them are examples of unabashed banditry by corporations with high-sounding names and the lowest possible business ethics. Many of them thrive because of the indifference or connivance of local authorities. Some are owned by the local politicians.

Everything is "proposed" in these real estate rookings—and most especially the "fantastic profits" alluded to in their four-color brochures. As one district attorney put it, "The paper is worth more than the land that's written on it."

Most persons from the Northeast and the Atlantic Coast tend to seek their recreational/second-homes in Florida and along the Gulf Coast. There are many splendid investment opportunities there, offered by reputable companies. General Development and Deltona are two such "old line" companies.

People from Chicago and the Midwest tend to prefer the beautiful Texas "hill country," the Ozarks, or New Mexico and Arizona. However, a good many Chicagoans do find their vacation pleasures in Florida, often along the Keys.

These seasonal migration patterns were established many years ago. Customarily they followed those earlier avenues of easy transport. Ships and rail lines sped New Yorkers to Florida. The Super Chief sped Midwesterners to New Mexico and Arizona and on to Southern California.

After World War II the greatly expanded commercial airlines followed roughly the same historical migration patterns. Then, with the advent of the commercial jetliner, those patterns began to change. Superhighways proliferated and were filled with climatized private cars and buses.

Americans, now the most mobile society on earth, began to break out of the old travel patterns and began to explore new places. Many of them traveled in the new "trailer homes" that permit a family to move its creature comforts from coast-to-coast and border-to-border—and beyond. Mobility, speed, comfort and curiosity combined with new affluence, and added leisure, to change vacation concepts.

National and state parks that were the "private preserves" of the relative few who lived close enough, or those who were rich enough to travel, became crowded. Parking was expanded to provide for the auto and trailer crowd. First, four parking lots in Yosemite Valley—and then forty. By 1970, thirty million holiday-minded Americans were on the move. Thousands of disappointed persons were turned away from state, county and national parks and campgrounds.

And the land developers *". . . saw the moving multitude and were joyful in their hearts."*

The inevitable result was the planned private vacation community as we know it now. It is in the best of these communities—and they offer a full spectrum of climate and activity—that we now find the best investments. No longer the province of the well-to-do, they range from Arizona's ultrasmart, spectacularly beautiful community of Carefree not far from Scottsdale, to North American Towns' remarkable "middle-income family" development at historic Fort Clark Springs directly across Highway 90 at Brackettville, Texas. Each offers the same natural and planned amenities and the same potential for both pleasure and profit.

Hugh Downs and Dick Van Dyke live in Carefree, Arizona. Some other happy people from the opposite side of the TV screen live at Fort Clark Springs—and the twain do meet in their mutual enjoyment of the unspoiled natural beauty of their respective communities.

We have not singled out these two developments for any particular purpose. In our travels around the country—indeed, the world—we have visited literally hundreds of second-home/recreational communities. Certainly some were better than others in the scope and quality of their planning. It is said that a man is known by the company he keeps. We would paraphrase that by saying that a company is known by the promises it keeps. Proposed amenities are really promises when they are used by salesmen as inducements to buy. As we shall see shortly, these promises are not always kept.

In choosing a recreational/second-home investment, the first thing to look into is the reputation of the developer. It may be an individual, a consortium or a corporation. Frequently, of late, the developing corporation will be part of a giant conglomerate that has discovered this huge new market and decided to exploit it. But whichever it is, the firm will have a record of achievement. *It is very important to know about that. It is also important to remember that "big" is not always "good."*

Having made certain that you know what sort of recreation and leisure living you *really* want, and having made certain that you are doing business with a *reputable developer who has ample resources to complete his end of the bargain,* the best time to buy is *early.*

For us this is not theory. We have demonstrated the wisdom of such a course in a number of places over the years. First, some twenty years ago at Fire Island, New York; later at Stuart, Florida; still later at Incline Village on the Nevada side of Lake Tahoe; and more recently at central Oregon's incredibly beautiful Sunriver. In each case, we were early purchasers—sometimes founding members.*

How does one find these ground-floor situations? First, select the areas that interest you. Next, invest a few dollars in subscriptions to the area's best local newspapers. Invariably, the advent of a new major development will be front-page news. Often it will rate editorial comment too. We pay close attention to editorial comment. On the whole, we find editors taking the long-range view toward these "outsiders" who come in with dazzling plans. Long since, they and their chambers of commerce and their tax assessors have found out that while short-term razzle-dazzle may stimulate the area for a while, in the end it can do great damage.

The announcement of a major new recreational development will be followed up with continuing announcements, advertisements and straight news stories. Some of these will be generated by the developer's public relations and sales promotion people. But it is easy to tell the difference between the "puff" and the "hard stuff." Some of the best editing and reporting in the country is found in our smaller newspapers.

If your interest lies in three areas, send the money for those subscriptions. What can it cost? Fifteen or twenty dollars a year? That's a very modest amount to pay in order to insure that you'll make a wise investment of from $10,000 to $50,000 and more of your hard-earned dollars.

Once you are on the trail of some promising developments, write to the company for its literature. If that arouses your interest, plan to visit the area. If your interest is heightened still more, follow these commonsense steps:

1. Make absolutely certain that you know what you want.

---

*See *The Simple Truth about Western Land Investment.*

2. Spend enough time in the area to be sure you've chosen the best deal for you. (You may not know until you've rented or leased for a season.)
3. Check out the developer with some "tough-minded" questions. If there is still a lingering doubt about representations, write to the Office of Interstate Land Sales Registration, Department of Housing and Urban Development, Washington, D.C. 20410. Ask if any complaints have been filed against the developer or the development. Make the same inquiry of the state Real Estate Commission.
4. Look carefully at what is *proposed* and what is *completed. Promises are cheap. Construction is not.* If the developer will not put it in writing, you're in the wrong place.
5. If everything seems to check out—*still take your time.* Don't rush into the deal. It will still be there in the morning. But if you should act hastily and suffer "buyer's remorse," in most states you'll have forty-eight hours to change your mind. In California you'll have two weeks. Actually, an ethical developer does not want you to move too quickly. He would rather have you be certain than sorry. A bad deal can be costly for him, too, and he certainly does not need a dissatisfied buyer going around spreading "infectious grumpitis."
6. Take the time to ask around in nearby communities. Talk to local bankers, the chamber of commerce, savings and loan people. Inquire into the development company's standing in the market either through a local stockbroker or your own.
7. Check the developer in Dun & Bradstreet. See if he has an acceptable financial rating. Your *banker* can do this for you.
8. Again, under no circumstances should you sign anything until you have thoroughly checked the *final* subdivision public report required by most state

real estate departments, and by the Office of Interstate Land Sales Registration of the U.S. Department of Housing and Urban Development—the HUD we read so much about. Pay special attention to those elements in the report that are *negative.* Demand clarification and bear in mind that the report probably covers only the *subdivision unit* then on sale, *not* the entire development. In the end the value of your purchase will depend largely on the overall value of the completed development. *That may take ten years or more.* Remember, promises that are not a formal, written part of the contract mean nothing. Remember also the cogent homily attributed to Samuel Goldwyn, "A verbal contract isn't worth the paper it's written on."

9. Pay close attention to the availability *and cost* of sewage treatment, adequate water, electricity, gas, telephone, road and street maintenance, storm drainage and taxes—and assessments, if any. Be sure to check the *possibility of future assessments* for the installation and maintenance of basic services as well as maintenance of recreational facilities. Double-check the answers against the public reports.

10. Future assessments and escalating taxes are two important factors to consider very carefully if you are planning to make your recreation home your retirement residence. Also, the proximity and quality of medical facilities are vitally important. *Unexpected assessments, rising taxes and costly, inadequate medical care can be disastrous if you expect to retire on a fixed income.**

---

*See the Cooleys' book, *How to Avoid the Retirement Trap,* Nash, 1972, for a full discussion of these and other dangers.

Many developers, in order to generate a cash flow from sales, will offer a "predevelopment special." The best of these are bargains offered to early purchasers who pay cash. Generally that means a 10 to 20 percent discount on the *retail* price of the homesite *before it is fully developed.* In effect, the developer is "paying you a bonus" to use *your cash* to help develop your property. That is all well and good if you can afford the cash, and if he has quoted you a "kosher" retail price.

An ethical developer will not tamper with the retail price once it has been set for the particular unit. But quite often similar lots in units developed later may actually retail at higher prices—a good break for you *if the development is completed as promised.*

In some instances, "predevelopment" discounts may be offered on a deferred payment basis, or on a short-term payout basis, if you pay cash within sixty to ninety days, let's say. Another option gives you discount privileges if you finance the homesite and then decide within a specified time that you wish to pay out the balance in cash.

Land contracts used to carry penalty clauses for paying up early. Some still do. Their purpose was to partially reimburse the developer for the loss of interest income if the contract did not run its full term. Otherwise, if he had a number of defaults, he might not be able to acquire clear title to the unit and therefore would not be able to convey title to those in the unit who did pay up in full.

But most developers prefer to use a "no penalty" clause as an added inducement to commit you to a sale in the first place. In other words, you may pay up the full amount at any time without being liable for the interest you would have paid on the unpaid balance over the contract's term.

Before you commit yourself to buy a piece of property—regardless of the reputation of the seller—it is wise to consult a knowledgeable attorney (not all attorneys are expert in real estate) to review the contract with you, particularly if the property is out of state. Realtors and brokers may not act as attorneys unless they have law degrees, and most do not. They may be right; they may actually know as much or more about real estate law as a competent attorney. But if you should find yourself in a bind you cannot run back to them. The best of them will refuse to counsel you in legal matters.

Remember also that no matter how "charming" these sales representatives may seem—and regardless of the licenses and degrees they may hold—you do not ask the person you purchase from to confirm the validity of your bargain. Listen to the reassurances, take notes, then double-check with the lawyer who has no ax to grind.

We would feel a bit silly stressing such obvious counsel over and over were it not for the fact that our files are sprinkled with tearful letters from people who got taken because "the salesman was so open and aboveboard that he just inspired confidence." Of course he did! That, and a thorough knowledge of his product and of human nature are his stock in trade. He may be as honest as the subdivision is large, but it is well to remember that where salespeople are concerned, there's a little bit of "con" in every pro. They may be telling you the truth. But you must make certain that they are telling you the *whole* truth.

When you are handed the real estate reports and the prospectus, you are being handed the *responsibility* for protecting yourself against all of the things the salespeople do *not* say. So long as they do not misrepresent their product, the buyer has little or no recourse if, too late, he finds some things in his signed contract that he has not clearly understood.

In order to make certain that the developer and his staff have no liability under such circumstances, the buyer is usually required to sign an affidavit stating that he *has* read the prospectus, the agreement and the reports, and *has* understood them.

We do not say that the language in the prospectuses is deliberately designed to be devious or to obfuscate. But we do say that we'd like to see a federal law requiring the conditions of a sale to be spelled out in the simplest possible language. Simplicity, clarity and accuracy are compatible objectives. There is no reason why a seller's obligations and a buyer's obligations cannot be stated simply and clearly. As a matter of fact, such clarity would probably inspire confidence and ease the way to a signed deal. At its worst, it would save everybody time in the event the deal did not suit the buyer. And time, they say, is money!

It is worth pointing out again how the historic patterns of internal migration in our country have affected the value of land. Accessibility by waterway, railroad and road has always been the key factor in predicting where values are apt to increase. Again, the 1970 census supplies corroborative testimony: While nonmetropolitan counties as a whole are growing *below* the national average, those nonmetropolitan counties *crossed by a throughway* and having a moderate size urban center (25,000 to 50,000 population) are growing more rapidly than ever. In fact, they are growing at the same rate as the national average—13 percent. Certainly logic would indicate that the "royal road to real estate profit" may be that new freeway. But as the young Reverend Hubert Stillwater Blessing observed in the novel *The Trouble with Heaven,* "It is possible to be logical without being right," which suggests that unless a buyer really does his homework, the new freeway may also be the road to a "royal shafting"!

Now, let's look at a few of the principal types of second-home recreational developments. As you'll see, they are a "mixed bag." They range from fee-simple trailer sites "a million miles from nowhere" to ultraelegant "club developments" only an hour or so from town. Their amenities are less a matter of variety than elaborateness. But whether they are planned for "prince or peasant," they all must have in common several basic qualities to be worth considering as profit-producing investments. When we've finished looking at the "mixed bag," those qualities should be evident.

5. *General view of historic Fort Clark Springs at Brackettville, Texas. Number 1, headwaters of Las Moras Creek. It originates in a huge fresh-water spring. Number 2, the old Second Cavalry stables, now refurbished for club members. Number 3, The Fort Theater, now remodeled for a combination movie and clubhouse. Number 4, the parade ground, now a pitch-and-putt golf course. Number 5, General Robert E. Lee's historic "court martial office." Fort Clark Springs is a living museum in an area of Texas just now coming into its own as an unparalleled year-round vacation and retirement spot.*

North American Towns of Texas, Inc. is the developer. [Photograph, courtesy of Zintgraff, San Antonio, Texas.]

6. *A new kind of "Light Brigade" charges along the company street at the old Second Cavalry headquarters at Fort Clark Springs. Developer N. K. Mendelsohn's meticulous sense of historicity virtually underwrites the preservation and enjoyment of the old fort's traditional values. Once indoctrinated, new owners become amateur curators of the "living museum" that is the entire area.*

7. *Newly completed Mexican "pueblito" at Fort Clark Springs, Texas. Club members may opt for an individual home site or buy one of the condominium-style residences included in the several "theme communities." [Photograph, courtesy of Zintgraff, San Antonio, Texas.]*

8. *Pasture land at Battle Creek Ranches. Obscured by clouds, is Mt. Lassen and the high country in the famous recreational area that borders the development. [Photograph by author.]*

9. *Ancient petroglyphs carved in the cliffs along Bear Creek in Battle Creek Ranches development east of Cottonwood, California. Co-author L.F.C., who rode through here as a boy with cattle drives, remembers talk that the prehistoric carvings were made by the predecessors of the Yahi tribe long before the coming of the white man.*

Local legend claims that the main carving depicts an ancient deluge; on the right, what is presumed to be a depiction of flood "cascades" finally merging into a winding stream. (Local legends are often very "unscientific!") Scholars now studying the symbols may come up with a version of their own.

10. Trout riffles on Lack Creek at Battle Creek Ranches. Typical homesite terrain on either side. In addition to being a fisherman's delight, the area is a rich hunting ground for rock hounds.

11. *Portion of refurbished Front Street, the "main drag" of historic Cottonwood, California. Rustic Battle Creek Ranch office in background. North American Towns has purchased the abandoned S.P. Railroad Station and donated it to the town. Local citizens are turning it into an impressive historical museum, filled with pioneer cattle, mining, and Indian artifacts.*

12. Early winter in Ball's Ferry Park, a five-acre picnic area on the Sacramento River donated to Shasta County by North American Towns of California. In the summer the deciduous California oaks are dense with new leaves, providing great pools of welcome shade. [Photograph by Gregory Iger, Bakersfield, California.]

13. *Model home at Tenneco's 3,200-acre Pine Mountain Club just 88 miles from downtown Los Angeles. Terrain runs from 4,600 feet to 8,800 feet. Every recreational amenity is available for year-round sport—golfing, water sports, winter sports, mountain climbing, and horseback riding are the favorites.*

As of December 1972, there were over 200 completed homes. Great care is taken in siting and design. Pine Mountain is ideally located for urban dwellers who want to get away from it all for a weekend or longer—any time of the year. [Photograph by Gregory Iger, Bakersfield, California.]

10.
The New Residential-Recreational Communities

It is hard to categorize these communities. Some of them are really self-contained cities. Many of them could be considered suburban communities. Others are out beyond the suburbs and provide peripheral shopping but rely on their proximity to metropolitan centers via high-speed freeways for major mercantile and medical services.

Generally this later category tends to contain a mix of full-time suburbanites who commute to the city to work and a large population of part-time vacationers. Sprinkled among these will be the affluent retirees, often high-ranking military personnel and their families and the resident artists and writers who have made it and can live where they please. An excellent example of such a community would be Lakeway, currently being created by the Alpert Investment Corporation and Connecticut Mutual on Lake Travis twenty-five miles west-northwest of Austin, Texas.

Less than a forty-minute drive to the state capitol building, Lakeway boasts purchasers from every state in the union and some twenty-six foreign countries. The owners' roster reads like a veritable *Who's Who Anywhere*. What brings them to Lakeway? After two full days of "snooping," it was easy to see that the development could quite literally be "all things to all people," with the obvious reservation that the people be well fixed financially.

In addition to a beautiful lake with sixty-five miles of wooded shoreline nestled in Texas's lovely "hill country," Lakeway's developers are at great pains to provide everything that a mere mortal could ask for. Activities range from just "settin' an' rockin' an' starin' at the view" to golfing on one—soon two—championship golf courses (are there any *other* kind?) to horseback riding, sailing, angling for Texas-sized fish or "angling" for a doubles match at the 100-acre Lakeway World of Tennis complex.

Lying within the overall Lakeway community, the World of Tennis is being developed by Lamar Hunt, Al G. Hill, Jr., and the Alperts, Robert and Maurice, of Dallas. They have designed the complex as "playing headquarters for World Championship Tennis," a name familiar to TV tennis buffs from coast to coast.

Each townhouse boasts its own private tennis court, and there are, in addition, a dozen other courts and an exhibition match stadium that can be expanded from 2,500 seats to 8,500, a contingency that will doubtless come in handy. Townhouses were selling in the $50,000 to $80,000 price range, as of November 1972, with no sale consummated until the prospective purchaser had been accepted as a member of the Tennis Club.

Thoughtful planning and complete architectural control have worked a minor aesthetic and ecological miracle throughout Lakeway. Residential lots are spacious—one-third to one-half acre. Minimum living space must be 1,500 square feet, exclusive of garage or carport. All homes must be compatible in design with other homes in the development but may not be a duplication of any existing home. Incredible enough, despite the general use of natural materials indigenous to the Texas hill country, each home manages a charming individuality. Or perhaps it is not incredible when one realizes that the average cost of a Lakeway single family residence is $72,000, including the lot.

Taken as a whole, Lakeway is a beautiful development, still expanding under a superior master plan that leaves natural terrain virtually undisturbed. It seems likely that if profits may also be reckoned in pleasure, as we suggested earlier, then most Lakeway owners have found themselves "double-barrel bargains," as one resident put it.

It must be clear from the average residential cost that a bargain at Lakeway does not mean "cheap." There is nothing inexpensive about the place, nor could there be if an owner expected to receive full value for dollars invested there.

Lakeway and other such communities (from Florida's Marco Island on the Gulf; South Carolina's Sea Pines Plantation on Hilton Head Island; and Stowe, Vermont's Notch Brook in the East to Utah's Snowbird less than thirty minutes from Salt Lake City; Arizona's Fountain Hills near Scottsdale; Nevada's Incline Village and California's Northstar at Lake Tahoe to Hawaii's Plantation Hale on the island of Kauai) stand at top of the price range. And still it is possible in Lakeway to buy a fully improved one-third to one-half acre lot on what is called a "secluded site" (no view of lake but one of wooded hills and canyons and possibly a segment of fairway) for less than $5,000* (or about half as much as unscrupulous "land butchers" have gotten for two and a half acres of raw jackrabbit land in other parts of the West and Southwest). But it is also possible to pay ten times that and more for a lakefront homesite.

In using Lakeway as an example, let us reemphasize that it is not our intention to recommend one area or one development over another. The developments identified by name in *Land Investment, U.S.A.,* were selected solely because they appear to represent excellent models of thoughtful planning, careful execution and administration. Again, those are basic qualities if an investment is to have any sort of pleasure and profit potential. Moreover, it must be clear that if we were to choose only two representative examples of fine recreational development from each state, this work would soon turn into a directory, and this is not its function.

---

*As of November 1972.

The best of these second-home or residential-recreational developments may vary widely in its *central attraction* such as a lake, river or ocean shoreline, or proximity to them. Some developments, such as Nevada's Incline Village on the north shore of Lake Tahoe, boast all of the usual amenities plus a famous "in-town" ski resort.

When we were asked to differentiate—to spell out the differences between the inland lake community, the river development, the ocean-oriented community and the all-year mountain community, we replied that beyond their central attractions there were none. All of the best developments have hotels or inns and good bars and restaurants. All of them have a wide variety of optional primary and basic secondary recreational facilities. Many owners enjoy the complete spectrum of seasonal sports from skiing to golfing, fishing, swimming, tennis, bicycling, hiking and riding. The ski buff is apt to lease out his place for the summer and the sun-worshipper may lease out for the winter. But with more and more leisure time, most younger families nowadays tend to make all-year use of their second homes.

It should be pointed out that the seasonal rental potential of a place, *if correctly assessed,* can be instrumental in allowing a young "on-the-way-up" family the luxury of a top-quality second home a bit sooner than they might be able to manage otherwise. To plan that way, in effect, is "buying on margin." Should business in general, or personal fortunes, take a downward turn, the buyer should be in a position to meet a "call."

It seems more prudent to rely on bonus rental income to pay incidental, not capital, expenses. Use rental income to pay taxes, maintenance, insurance and club dues. And check your tax man about depreciation write-offs and other advantages in case of a sale.

It is hard indeed to go into the best of these developments without being sorely tempted to stretch finances a bit—a temptation that salesmen are well aware of, and that few can resist exploiting. As the eager one-legged forty-niner was reported to have said to the madam of a San Francisco bordello, "Jes' open the door, Ma'am. I kin git upstairs by myself. There's times when a man kin overlook his infirmities!"

While Lakeway might be said to have two equally important central attractions—Lake Travis and golf (and now tennis)—there are other highly successful residential-recreational communities of approximately the same size and in the same economic bracket that do well with just one.

In Southern California, about a ninety-mile freeway drive south of Los Angeles or a twenty-mile drive north of San Diego, lies 5,000-acre *La Costa*. Within sight of long reaches of Pacific Ocean shoreline, La Costa's master plan will eventually provide for 7,000 single-family and condominium residences.

Substitute two championship golf courses and nearby beaches for a large lake, add absolutely everything else necessary to satisfy the merest whim of the weekend sybarite of either sex, and you'll get an elementary idea of the La Costa version of "the good life." If all of this should pall (despite a liberal sprinkling of top movie and TV names) it is a leisurely ten-minute drive to the Del Mar racetrack where, during the season, one can make riskier investments, limited only by the player's faith and finances.

Certainly La Costa's central attraction is its championship golf course. (As this is being written, a second course is about to be completed.) Rated as one of the finest golf courses in North America, it measures 7,200 yards of all but insoluble problems for the novice and presents a worthy challenge to the world's greatest pros.

Just as Lakeway World of Tennis can boast world championship matches in that sport, so La Costa is the scene of such major golf events as the PGA Tournament of Champions, the CBS Golf Classic, the Haig Scotch Mixed Foursome Championship, the American Airlines Astrojet Tournament, and others.

At all of the major residential-recreational developments we visited all over the United States and in Europe and Mexico, too, prices of homesites and condominiums tended to increase rapidly. Almost always these price increases were initiated arbitrarily by the developers and were referred to as increases in value. But it is worth pointing out that there can be a vast difference between higher price and greater value. *Price, in this case, is the figure a developer places on his product. But real value must be measured in terms of what a purchaser can realize in the open market in the event a resale is necessary.*

As tens of thousands of unwary purchasers of parcels in unanchored subdivisions in the West, Southwest and in parts of Florida learned too late, the bargains they hastened to get, before the developer's arbitrary price increase went into effect, not only could not be resold at the original "low, low introductory price" but could not be resold at any price—for no valid market existed. (More on those pressure techniques later.)

In a well-done project there may be arbitrary price increases in subsequent units of the development. In fact, we know of no developers who do not use the device to stimulate sales. There is nothing wrong with these "inducements" if the increased price of the land reflects a comparable increase in value. Again, *such an increase does not translate into real value unless a seller's market develops as the result of the excellence of the project*—in short, unless all the factors are present to initiate the "better mousetrap" syndrome.

How can a buyer make certain that price and value are realistically related? As we examine the various investments available, the value building factors will become apparent. They are not difficult to find, and they are easy to understand and evaluate. Perhaps you'll begin to get a clue from what we have written about *Lakeway* and *La Costa.* In both of those residential-recreational developments we talked to owners who had bought their units early and had either sold at very respectable net profits within three years, or who are still refusing tempting offers.

Usually the lots or units that increase in value fastest are those with preferred locations such as sites with views, or close to a recreational center, or overlooking the "central attraction"—the lake, river, beach, the fairway or whatever. In large developments there may be several such central attractions to be built later—two golf courses, for instance. The first investors usually will have attained the preferred positions the first time around; but there will be excellent, if not comparable, opportunities close by the newer activity centers. If the developer checks out, there is little risk in taking an option on a future lot that appeals to you. But if there is any doubt in your mind, go to a real estate broker in the area who is not connected with the development and price *comparable* land.

Lakeway and La Costa, as we have seen, are developments within easy freeway access of major metropolitan centers. We believe it may be useful to look at two more examples of well-planned, second-home, residential-recreational developments that are situated some distance from large metropolitan centers. One is Sunriver, Oregon, some 175 miles southeast of Portland and 157 miles east-southeast of the capital city of Salem.

The other, mentioned earlier, is Fort Clark Springs, Texas, 119 miles southwest of San Antonio, and literally just across the highway from Brackettville. Both developments have several interesting points in common. Both occupy the sites of historical military establishments, and both direct their appeal to a somewhat broader economic range.

Sunriver occupies 5,500 acres of meadow and timberland on the eastern slope of the Cascade Range. The area was once the famed Camp Abbot of the U.S. Army Corps of Engineers. Fifteen miles south of the busy commercial center of Bend, the development encompasses heavily timbered slopes and open meadowland, several thousand acres of which have been set aside in a permanent wildlife preserve by developer John Gray. Gray, an extraordinary Oregon industrialist, seems well on the way to realizing his long cherished dream of a residential-recreational resort in which people of "all walks" can live compatibly with nature.

The American Home magazine's writers visited Sunriver and studied its master plan. Later, when they sought words to describe the area, they said, with no fear of exaggeration, "It is a lyrically lovely land . . ." Moved to be more specific, they called Sunriver ". . . the healthiest new town in America."

Certainly we would not seriously question that description although, after visiting many beautiful "all-year" second-home resort developments, we believe it might be more accurate to say ". . . *one of the three or four* healthiest new towns in America."

It is entirely accurate to say that no natural setting could be more varied and spectacularly beautiful; and no master plan we have seen is more thoughtfully conceived to provide open spaces, greenbelts, communication channels and easily accessible recreation and service complexes.

Surrounded on three sides by the Deschutes National Forest and bisected by eight and one-half miles of the lovely Deschutes River, Sunriver is Oregon State at its most beautiful, and residential-recreational development at its highest art.

Homesites, with all utilities underground and three-stage sewage treatment that processes waste water into potable water for a six-acre supplementary wildlife resource, range in price from $6,450 to $21,500.*

Dwellings range in price from rustic ranch cabins in the $20,000 class to custom homes that cost $200,000 and more. Sunriver's condominium complexes are among the most interesting we have seen. There are two championship golf courses, fifteen miles of protected blacktop bicycle trails, a 5,000-foot surfaced airstrip with flight headquarters and tie-down facilities, a marina where canoes and outboards may be rented or berthed for those fishermen or just plain paddlers who wish to explore the thirty-five rapid-free miles of river accessible from the development.

The altitude at Sunriver is 4,200 feet which means there is snow in the winter; but it seldom exceeds a total of 36 inches for the season and individual snowfalls do not stay on the

---

*As of January 15, 1973.

ground for long periods. Just under an hour's drive is Mt. Bachelor which dominates the view to the west from Sunriver. It is here that the U.S. Olympic Ski Team does much of its training on some of the finest slopes in America. Two other ski facilities are nearby and all are easily accessible over all-year roads.

The Deschutes National Forest offers hundreds of miles of U.S. Forest Service roads for exploring; and one may ride horseback for months on end without retracing a trail.

The forest is one of the richest wildlife sanctuaries in America with hunting and fishing strictly controlled. In addition, Sunriver has its own full-time resident naturalist who not only tends to the preservation of the abundant and varied indigenous wildlife that inhabits the development's private sanctuaries, but also conducts field trips into the surrounding country. These expeditions are enormously popular with both children and adults.

On the whole, it is fair to say that in "this lyrically lovely land" John Gray and his new partner, Connecticut Mutual Life Insurance, are creating an extraordinary residential-recreational resort community.

We have talked about "second-home recreational communities" and "residential-recreational communities" and now, "residential-recreational-resort communities." Essentially they are the same except that those anticipating a high proportion of full-time residents (above and beyond the necessary merchants and service personnel) and, in addition, offering a full range of purely resort facilities, fall into this latter category. Properly, Lakeway (and developments such as Incline Village and Northstar at Lake Tahoe) should be in this category too. Particularly, since its beautiful inn is being doubled in size to take care of summer vacationers, most of whom come to the "hill country" to escape the heat and humidity of the Gulf Coast cities.

That brings us back to Texas and Fort Clark Springs close to the Mexican border and the new Amistad Reservoir just forty minutes down Highway 90. The 70,000-acre Amistad (Friend-ship) Lake—half in Mexico and half in the United States—is one of the most important new recreation areas on the North American continent.

Since prehistoric times an extraordinary crystal-clear spring of fresh water has welled up in a dense grove of native oak and pecan. The stream it forms, called Las Moras Creek, flows leisurely through 3,000 acres of picturesque woods and meadows and eventually finds its way to the Rio Grande some twenty miles distant. Known to the Spanish *exploradores* in the sixteenth century, and to the trappers and traders who came through the area two centuries later, the spring and its woods were continually peopled with the adventurers who built the West.

In 1851 the United States Army judged it an ideal base for its Indian-chasing Fourth Cavalry. A major frontier post was estab-lished there and designated as Fort Clark.

As writers we are tempted to devote some pages to the colorful and historically significant events that took place in and around the fort. Suffice it to say that such events were numerous and the fort's commanding officers included such illustrious names as General Robert E. Lee, General George Patton and General Jonathan Wainwright. General Lee's log-and-wattle court-martial quarters still stand as do the limestone residences of Generals Patton and Wainwright, together with many other original buildings.

Following World War II, Fort Clark passed into private hands and became a millionaire sportsmen's hunting preserve. In 1971, North American Towns of Texas purchased the entire property complete with all of the historic military installations and began a restoration program and new development under the name, Fort Clark Springs.

It would take a remarkable man enjoying remarkable good fortune to acquire the 2,699-acre oasis that was old Fort Clark. And it would take an even more remarkable developer to realize the significance of such a place and determine not only to restore and preserve the important historical structures but to develop there a second-home-recreational community that fits compatibly into less than 25 percent of the land. It seems apparent that Fort Clark and adjoining Brackettville, as well as Texas, found such a man in the unlikely person of a thoughtful one-time New York sociologist, N. K. Mendelsohn, whose dissatisfaction with the deterioration of American urban life led him, twenty years earlier, to plan two new western cities from scratch.

Motivated by a scholar's interest in detail and respect for history and armed with a wealth of wisdom acquired from earlier ventures, Mr. Mendelsohn set out to create a rich recreational environment that "nonrich" families could afford. In addition to the natural and in-built assets, North American Towns has under construction all of the recreational amenities found in the most expensive resorts.

"What we are trying to establish at Fort Clark Springs," says N. K. Mendelsohn, "is a community that will make it possible for middle-income families to have a second home within their means, and that means in the lower price range we must deliver some housing in the neighborhood of $10,000."

When we visited the development in the late fall of 1972, the Mendelsohn promise seemed well on the way to being kept. Housing, which will take up no more than 600 of the 2,699 acres, will be scattered around the four square miles of the wooded development in six *pueblitos* or "little towns."

Mindful of the colorful past, each of the new residential complexes will reflect a period in Texas's history. Fort Clark has lived under six flags—that of Spain, France, Mexico, the Republic of Texas, the Confederate States of America and the United States of America. The designers, Smith and Williams of Pasadena, California, are taking great care to see that each of these residential centers is authentic in external appearance. As a result, Fort Clark Springs will become a sort of living "theme park." There seems little doubt that if the development fulfills its objectives, some 8,000 families will eventually live or vacation in one of the most interesting and unusual environments we have seen anywhere.

The smallest of the dwellings runs somewhere around 600 square feet and is patently intended for weekend outings or for summer vacation facilities in which modern but minimal accommodations are required for a small family.

In the club concept that N. K. Mendelsohn has set up, a purchaser acquires a membership that carries with it a parcel of land large enough to build a second home containing upward of 2,000 square feet. It is anticipated that there will be many such dwellings. The locale offers such variety of activity that a number of families purchasing club memberships are planning to spend their retirement years at "the Springs" also. Planned into the community is an area of mobile homes. All utilities are underground and there are two modern waste-treatment plants.

A point of particular interest was the limitation on the number of membership homesites that may be purchased by one owner. The limit is three to discourage speculators from taking property off the market and holding it, undeveloped, a major problem that has beset many recreational developments.

Too often the developer doesn't care who buys how much so long as sales are good. But when that condition is allowed to exist, it is the buyer (who has invested in the improvements needed to make his home livable) who is the loser. A few scattered dwellings in a 10,000-acre development that is five to ten years old is a discouraging sight for a prospective new customer. Most will wonder why nothing has happened, think twice and walk away. N. K. Mendelsohn has charged Fred G. Johnston and his sales staff with the responsibility for seeing that this situation does not happen at Fort Clark Springs. If they are successful, it will mean unusual protection of present and future values for the owners.

In advertising their so-called "standard attractions" in second-home recreational communities, developers have a tendency to give equestrian centers the "once-over lightly" treatment, except in such equestrian-oriented projects as The Country at Diamond Bar Ranch and San Diego Country Estates with its International Equestrian Center (to name but two with major riding facilities out of the dozens we have visited).

Those developers who have placed primary emphasis on equestrian facilities have cannily taken advantage of a growing recreational trend that is placing horse training, breeding and riding in the forefront along with golf, skiing, boating and tennis.

In 1972 Equestrian Consultants, Inc., of Menlo Park and Portugese Bend, California, estimated an 8 million horse population in the United States, up from fewer than 3 million in 1959. The vast majority—perhaps as many as 95 percent of these animals—are being purchased for the pleasure of riding them.

Far from confining their choices to Western "cow ponies" and quarter horses, the owners are showing a profound interest in the older and technically more difficult "English School" of riding, and their mounts range from the lowly Western "cayuse" to the noblest Arabian thoroughbred and "leggy" Irish jumper.

Because of its military cavalry background, North American Towns' Fort Clark Springs is unique in this respect. The old cavalry stables have been restored to top condition, and George Wyrick, senior cavalry instructor at the fort for forty years, is in charge of the facilities and the mounts.

The development maintains a well-broken *caballada* of saddle animals to which private owners are adding their own fine stock. If the present trend continues, projections place the U.S. horse population at around 14 million head by 1980.

Quiet, smog-free and dependable, it would seem that the horse is about to win a signal victory over the horseless carriage, at least for a few weeks out of the year. And there is another advantage: Nobody has been able yet to compost hydrocarbons; but the "exhaust emissions" from Old Dobbin have long since proved their worth in the rose garden. More than that, there are few more rewarding leisure activities than several hours on a good animal, walking, pacing, jogging, loping, or galloping along wooded bridle trails. It is not surprising that, old tradition aside, more millions of Americans are finding in ownership of saddle animals a means of temporary retreat to yesteryear's "good life."

14. *This is the residence of Hugh Downs, distinguished TV personality, at Carefree, Arizona. This development and the adjoining one, The Boulders, are among the most exciting and well-planned we have seen. Many accomplished men and women in the arts and communications maintain residences at Carefree. Famed news commentator, Paul Harvey, broadcasts nationally from his residence there.*

15. Lee Morrison Cooley, with sales representative Tom Parmenter, "staking out our claim" on a beautiful 1/3-acre lot at Sunriver. All utilities, including sewer, are underground. The site is ready for building. A $12.00 monthly fee maintains all of the amenities held in common by the Property Owners' Association. There is no charge for the glorious view of Mt. Bachelor in the background. The U.S. Olympic Ski Team trains here. And, just "down the street," is some of the best fishing in the United States! (We made up our minds very quickly at Sunriver—with a minimum of "buyer's remorse.")

16. One of the many underpasses on the fifteen miles of protected bike paths at Sunriver, Oregon.

In winter, these paths make ideal "trails" for cross-country ski touring. Motorized vehicles are not permitted. [Photograph by Art Hupy, Seattle, Washington.]

17. *Aerial view of lodge and recreational complex at Sunriver, Oregon, 15 miles south of Bend. In the lower right, the first of the condominium apartments are visible. A rental service permits owners to derive income from their furnished apartments when they are not in residence. A management organization, operated by Sunriver, oversees a complete hotel service for those owners who wish to rent out their condominiums by the day, weekend, month, or season. Little Deschutes River winds through the background at edge of Deschutes National Forest, which surrounds Sunriver on three sides, providing extraordinary privacy. (In the background, Mt. Bachelor, of course!) [Photograph courtesy of Robert Lindsay's Associates, Eugene, Oregon.]*

18. *A Sunriver, Oregon, family begins a day of cross-country ski touring. For the more ambitious, the lifts at Mt. Bachelor are just a short drive to the west. [Photograph courtesy of Powers Photos, Tigard, Oregon.]*

19. Closeup of The Sunriver Lodge, which also houses two gourmet restaurants, a golf shop, and numerous other shops and boutiques. Guests register at the Lodge for their stays in rental condominiums. The entire 5,000-acre development is a wild game preserve overseen by Sunriver's resident naturalist . . . which accounts for the "relaxed" Canadian geese! Thousands of geese and ducks "weekend" here on their way south.

20. *"Canoe Club" and marina on the Deschutes River, Sunriver, Oregon. Thirty or more miles of rapids-free water make this a fine recreational facility. For skilled anglers, the fishing is among the most sporting in the country. Junior Isaac Waltons may prefer fishing for smaller fry in Sunriver's several lakes and ponds. [Photograph courtesy of Powers Photos, Tigard, Oregon.]*

21. *A typical single-family residence at Sunriver, Oregon.*
   Construction averages $22.00 per square foot. The workmanship of local contractors seems excellent. All homes are "climatized" for all-year comfort since most families who come to Sunriver from Portland and other urban areas use their second homes during most of the year. [Photograph by author.]

22. *An impromptu regatta on Lake Travis. Every conceivable water sport is enjoyed at Lakeway including a contest to catch the incredibly large native catfish—an international table delicacy.*

23. *The Great Hall at Sunriver, Oregon. Once the Army Corps of Engineers' recreation hall, it is now the focal point of indoor recreational activities at the popular second-home resort area. The scene of motion pictures, theatrical presentations, dances and special dinners, the Great Hall is seldom vacant! [Photograph by Joseph Van Warmer, Salem, Oregon.]*

24. *Aerial view of Lakeway on Lake Travis, near Austin, Texas.*
Shown, are the Lakeway Inn and surrounding cottages, with Marina and Yacht Club in foreground and residences in the background. Only a small part of the community is visible here. Since this photo was taken, the inn is being expanded greatly to meet the rising demand for accommodations. [Photograph by Joseph Van Warmer, Salem, Oregon.]

25. *One of the scores of unique and luxurious homes at Lakeway. Over-looking the lake, the hill country, and the fairways, no two homes are identical. Strict architectural control is maintained and no cutting and filling of land is permitted to establish homesites. (How the authors wish their own Southern California planners displayed such forethought!)*

26. Green on one of the two championship golf courses at Lakeway. (The Texas-style "Aerial Golf Cart" dropped in on the nearby airstrip for a friendly foresome!)

27. One of the attractions of Chet Huntley's Big Sky resort is the top-rated trout stream which meanders through the Meadow Village area and the golf course. Golfers, who may also be avid trout fishermen, may try their luck in the top trout waters of the West Fork while they let a foursome or two pass by.

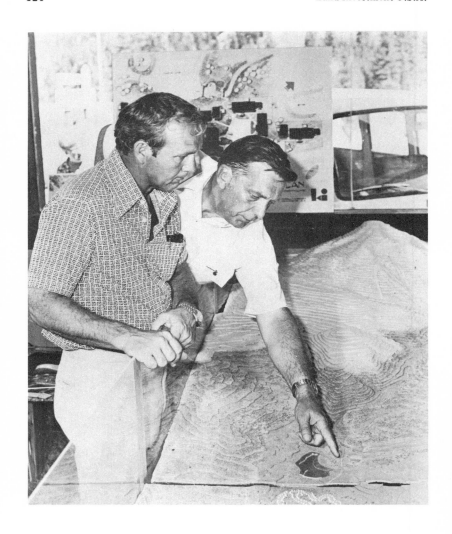

28. Chet Huntley and Arnold Palmer explore a diorama of the entire Big Sky resort and leisure area. The firm, Course Design, a division of Arnold Palmer & Associates, designed the 18-hole golf course which is the focal point of home sites and condominiums in Big Sky's Meadow Village.

29. Chet Huntley supervising the start of his own residence at Big Sky.

11.
Finding Your Own
Second-Home Place

"I would never buy in one of those big developments!" vowed a friend of ours who prides himself on being a rugged individualist. "Why should I pay a developer a big fat profit to supply me with five out of six things that I'll never use?"

We do not know whether our friend has answered that question satisfactorily for himself and his family yet. When last we heard from him, he and his wife and their two teenage boys were still roaming the country, looking. We gave him a list of things to look out for—questions that should be asked by any buyer of any land anywhere—and sent him on his way with a rabbit's foot for good measure.

In the meantime, for three reasons, we ourselves are happy to pay our pro rata share of the new facilities we do not normally use. First, when we do play golf it costs less on our course than it would if we managed to wangle guest cards at some other club. Second, because a number of other facilities are immediately available, we have tried them. The result? We have added several interesting new activities (and friends) to our recreational repertoire. Third, we know that preplanning has guaranteed us the zoning and orderly development that does so much to enhance pleasure and value. Nobody will be able to build a shack or put up a fried chicken stand next to us.

However, we acknowledge that many people, such as our friend and his family, prefer to "nest in" somewhere away from it all. They may well become part of the new breed of nomads which we'll discuss further on in the chapter "The New RVRs."

Because there are so many options in choosing a second-home locale, we should remind ourselves again that, for the moment we are still considering places primarily orientated toward family recreation.

A buyer who eschews the preplanned development may be faced with a more difficult problem now. First of all, the second-home recreational boom has created a seller's market in most of the desirable places from coast to coast. That means suitable land, if it can be found, will probably be far more expensive now. Moreover, because of the nationwide concern of conservationists for our remaining open space, local county and state authorities may have placed new restrictions on such land that would make it uneconomical for a single owner.

This holds true not only for many areas in Florida where improvement costs are prohibitive on a small parcel to make it conform to new county and state regulations; but it is equally true of some of the most "problem-free" land in the country.

For example, adventurous members of our family who wanted to control the whole thing themselves—who wanted "to get back to nature" on their own terms—drove north toward Oregon along California's spectacular coastal road, Cabrillo Highway. After passing a number of new second-home "country club" communities including the much publicized ultra-elegant Sea Ranch, they came to the upper end of Mendicino County.

There, after following our counsel to stop in and talk with the "locals," they got on the track of a 160-acre farm lying along a partly timbered slope overlooking the Pacific. The view was breathtaking. In August, so was the weather. They fell in love with the place, negotiated a reasonable deal, went into escrow and concluded the purchase around the first of November, 1972.

During the escrow period they employed a surveyor to break up the farm into a number of smaller parcels that they planned to sell to friends. The idea was to install a common water system, bulldoze ranch roads to each parcel and bring in electrical power along the rights of way. Since the parcels would be in excess of 20 acres each, cesspools would handle the sewage. In addition to the sizable cash commitment needed for the land purchase, several thousand dollars were spent on drawing up preliminary subdivision plans.

Much earlier in the year, when California's famous Coastal Zone Conservation Act, know as Proposition 20, was first discussed, we pointed out to our determined family members that if the bill passed they might not be able to pursue their plans. The reaction was predictable.

"Listen," they countered, "that proposition will never pass in a thousand years! Why, if it did, a billion dollars worth of coastline development would be knocked out. The real estate lobby is too powerful to let that happen."

To make a sad story short, Proposition 20 was passed—resoundingly. Development within the prescribed coastal strip was stopped cold, and a lot of political pundits retreated from the battle, both bloody and bowed.

The most desirable one-third of their new land lies well within the 1,000 yard "cordon sanitaire" in which no development may now take place. As things presently stand, unless restrictions are relaxed sometime in the future, these members of our family are the reluctant sole owners of a beautiful 160 acre former farm that they can't use for any other purpose. More than a little contrite, they now agree that it would have been wiser to buy a small existing retreat, fix up the old house and enjoy the serenity of the area without trying to add to their pleasure by making a financial killing. If they can find a buyer and "get out even," that is what they plan to do. The new law will not make that easy.

A minor land subdivision law recently passed by the California legislature to thwart the willy-nilly breaking up of small farms places a number of other would-be subdividers in much the same sort of bind—unless they are willing to go through the complicated and costly process of filing a formal subdivision map and risk an official turndown.

Both laws generated much legal turmoil, and a political process, known euphemistically as "clarification," is now going on. In the meantime, the new owners of the unsubdividable land must pay taxes which continue to rise despite the status quo that permits no new development.

The lesson to be learned here is simple: In the present political climate it is probably unwise for an amateur investor to buy more land in recreational areas than he needs personally in the hope that he can become a sort of a mini-subdivider, and sell off enough parcels to pay for his own piece and show some cash profit to boot. This can still be done in some high-growth areas if the timing is right. Generally speaking, though, what was once a fairly simple practice can now be a hazardous one.

The rugged individualist who is tempted to go it alone should make certain of both state and county restrictions before taking the plunge. If the seller is a rancher or farmer who has been scratching out a bare living and hoping to get out from under, he may not tell the buyer everything he knows; and then too, he himself may not know.

A canny investor will take the trouble to find out if he can legally and economically implement his plans for two reasons: to protect his own position, and to improve his bargaining edge if new regulations are only contemplated but have not been passed.

Most new land regulations are not retroactive beyond some reasonable date. But a buyer, armed with information that laws are "in the works" that can actually lower the value of the seller's land in its present use category, can often drive a better bargain by being willing to move quickly. The psychology is the reverse of that used by the high-pressure salesman who urges you to buy now "before the price goes up." It is, rather, "Sell now—before the value (to you) goes down!" Lamentably, it usually works.

Boom areas are particularly sensitive to conservationists' attention. Lately, when local authorities recognize the symptoms of a developing boom, they hasten to move first before the conservationists begin to apply political squeeze. In effect, they are positioning themselves so they can say to their constituency, "These conservationist people are a bit late poking their noses into our area. Look what we've already done with our new ordinances." It's a case of "If you cain't fight 'em off altogether, j'ine 'em halfway!" And that usually works, too.

Perhaps no inviting rural area better typifies what happens when investors "discover" an area than does Woodstock, New York.

Long an art colony famed for its theater, its concerts and its local craftsmen, Woodstock gained the erroneous distinction of being the scene of the world's most notorious rock "happening," an event that actually took place sixty-five miles to the north, in a Sullivan County cow pasture.

Woodstock's good name was dragged into the unprecedented "musical orgy," as some papers termed it, because the young producers were said to have been Woodstockers.

Some of the old-timers date the beginning of the "land rush" to the Woodstock rock concert's movie version that brought the place's name to prominence all over the United States and Canada. Unaware that they were not visiting the actual scene, a number of vacationers and weekenders sought out the tiny Ulster County village one hundred throughway miles north of New York City, and were enchanted by its quaintness and its unspoiled, unpolluted beauty.

Pioneer Woodstock real estate broker Irving Kalish, speaking to us from his modest office on Mill Hill Road, estimated that in the past decade the population of Woodstock has grown from "several hundred to about forty-five hundred now."

From a long time New York City friend who has recently built a second home in Woodstock, we received the following letter dated the day after Thanksgiving 1972:

> In Woodstock itself, and just close by, I hear land is now going for from $3,000 to $10,000 an acre in the real estate offices. When we bought up here about five years ago, we were shown a few choice pieces at $3,000 an acre in town. But it was still possible to get larger pieces at $1,000 an acre.
>
> Not any more! Although if you know people who are unaware of the change—and you're lucky—you can get some larger pieces for $2,000 an acre. (The completion of the New York Throughway had a marked effect on Woodstock land values, also. Accessibility again!)

Our friend unwittingly elucidated a basic principle in land investment. *If you have researched an area thoroughly and the signs are all "go" for investment, you may be able to find a bona fide bargain in a transaction with a "local" who is too close to the land to see the value.* And bargains may also be had from estates that need to be settled quickly.

The principle of "people pressure" is presently operating in Woodstock, too. Our friend's letter continues:

> If you add another hour of travel time from the throughway exit, it seems you can still get large tracts of good land from the old farmers for $500 an acre, which, when divided into three- and five-acre lots, will go for $1,000 an acre and up.

When we expressed some concern about ecological considerations and protective zoning in the Woodstock area, Mr. Kalish indicated that the town itself had long since imposed rigid zoning minimums.

With the exception of some three-quarter acre business sites downtown, the minimum plot for a single-family residence is two acres. "Many of the subdividers are making larger minimums—from three to five acres," he said.

Except for a small downtown area served by a local water system, the individual residents sink their own wells, at an average cost of $2,500. Including access road, water and sewage disposal, an owner may expect to pay around $5,000 over the cost of the homesite. Waste is handled by septic tanks which have more than ample leach fields on the large homesites.

So far as the surrounding area is concerned, Ulster County's Planning Board is presently at work on zoning regulations that will prevent the "ruination" of the area by commercialism.

Not all of the residents are old-timers. In Kingston, a twenty-minute drive away, an IBM computer plant employs approximately 6,000 people, some of whom have chosen Woodstock as a permanent residence.

It is also worth noting that, for the time being at least, Woodstock and the surrounding area have resisted the construction of cluster-type condominium dwellings and apartments. Residents feel that the intrusion of high-density structures will alter the character of the lovely village. Conservationist groups are also joining in the opposition to the outside promotional developers. If the protective low-density high-acreage zoning prevails, Woodstock's real estate investments may well prove to have been even better than suspected.

It is difficult, in citing examples, to differentiate between what is essentially a summer second-home colony such as Woodstock and a number of similar picturesque villages in New Jersey, Pennsylvania, Maryland and Virginia, and in Michigan, Wisconsin and Arkansas as well. Once discovered, these places also tend to become year-around communities for the thousands who are affluent enough to change their life-style or retire to the Florida Keys, the Southwest, the West or the snow country.

Twenty years ago when we used to ski at Stowe, Vermont, and warm ourselves at The Lodge, then owned by Bunny and George Morrell, it was possible to buy "stony field" farmland in the area for $100 an acre. (And we think back now with some regret at how many times Bunny and George urged us to do so.)

Of course, the same situation was true then in Utah, Colorado, Nevada, New Mexico, California, Montana, Wyoming or any place that provided cool summer mountain vacationing and superb winter ski conditions. It is not easy to foresee and assess the trends that will alter the nature of our leisure activities. Few people predicted the resurgence of the bicycle and tennis craze we are witnessing now.

Fortunately for the average small-land investor, it is not necessary, or even desirable, to attempt to "lead" the trend. It is far better to let the big developers who have vast research capabilities make the first move. After you see how they are faring in an area, there is still an opportunity for the rugged individualist to come in and buy what will prove, in time, to have been a bargain. That is the "piggyback" technique. It works very well for those who remain alert to change.

30. *Architects' concept of the Lakeway World of Tennis now under construction at Lakeway, near Austin, Texas. Conceived by Robert and Maurice Alpert, Al G. Hill, Jr., and Lamar Hunt, this must be the most ambitious and promising project in the annals of professional sport and recreation industry development. A partnership between World Championship Tennis and the Alpert Corporation, this residential recreational club will be the most advanced of its kind in the world.*

31. Final design of residences under construction. Charlton Heston and James Franciscus are among the early members, according to management. Each group of residences has its own private courts in addition to the "tennis bowl" where amateur and professional tournaments are held. Residences range from a 2-bedroom, 2½-bath "A" unit at $60,000 to a 3-bedroom, 3½-bath "D" unit at $84,500. Monthly dues depend upon resident status, but average $20 plus an initiation fee.

12.
John & Jane Dough: The New "Country Gentlepeople"

We have talked about modest acreage in the country and about the individualists who seek solitude well beyond the established communities. Even though they constitute only a minority—fewer than 300,000 who own their own working farms—there are far more people who dream of being able to buy a small place in the country that can be operated efficiently enough to pay for itself or at least pay taxes, upkeep, and perhaps throw off a little toward capital obligations after depreciation of structures and equipment.

Of this country-gentlemen minority, few actually stay on the property full time and operate it. Most use the places as occasional retreats and lease the land out to tenant farmers. Fifty such owners, interviewed from Maine to Washington, admitted that returns had been disappointing. Some owners had managed to realize a little money to apply on payments, taxes and maintenance. Most of the benefits came as indirect "profit" through tax shelters—savings on taxes as a result of depreciation schedules. Too often, neighboring farmers who sharecrop the land for the city owners do not appear to do much more than get by. The absentee owner has few alternatives and usually must accept his tenant's word.

At best, farming is a gamble in which Mother Nature (who, as we know from TV, is not to be fooled for long) holds the winning cards. Bitter family experience has taught us about those gambles. An unprecedented freeze in our Northwest apple country wipes out thousands of acres of mature trees in an hour's time, sap freezes internally, trunks and limbs of beautiful trees literally explode and split along their length—a decade of expense and back-breaking labor has gone for nothing!

Name the place and name the crop. A dozen witnesses will appear to corroborate the reality of the farmers' gamble. It was always so. Even Florida is not immune.

We have dear friends in the Orlando area who counted on their modest citrus grove to supplement the money needed to pay for their second home and retirement acreage. A freeze wiped them out. Unable to hang on, they gave up the place— *two years before Disney World* sent values skyrocketing for miles around.

We feel that the farm of the "gentlepersons" is not for the average investor for two reasons: Such places seldom live up to their optimistic income projections; and even if one is able to hang on for a while, new zoning and surrounding development inevitably will drive up taxes and improvement assessments, probably beyond the owner's ability to pay—*especially if one must live on a fixed income.*

These farms and *ranchitos* are "playthings" and tax shelters and good investments for the affluent buyer who wants to take a future position in valuable real estate while he and his family enjoy the good rural life during vacations and holidays. Most of us who yearn to see things grow are far better off with an acre or two in a less precarious land investment. Most of us can take as much pride in an apron full of beefsteak tomatoes from the backyard as we can from a truckload of lug boxes from the "south forty."

However, if you are "hell-bent" on getting back to the land, you will need the services of a reputable broker who specializes in small farms; and, also, the counsel of a skilled tax accountant or attorney who can guide you through the intricacies of depreciation schedules, deductible improvements on soil-conditioning and water sources. If you will do that—and if you will be patient for a decade or so—it could be that you'll convert those tax advantages into a respectable capital asset. Moreover, if you have chosen your farm "in the path of progress," you may get run over by a megalopolis in which case the "highest and best use" of your farmland may be a residential subdivision which, as we will see a little later, can make a "gentleperson farmer" very well off even after taxes.

13.
The "Prefab Farm" as an Investment

Many years ago, when the Southern Pacific and Santa Fe Railroads were promoting immigration to the West over their new transcontinental tie-in systems, some perceptive "horseback" psychologists foresaw the appeal a small "place in the sun" would have to hard-working, winter-bound Midwestern farmers.

Working with horticulturists through land-company subsidiaries, they set out thousands of five- and ten-acre citrus groves in Southern California and offered them on easy terms that included free transportation for the entire family.

When enterprising local promoters saw how well the idea worked, they too began to buy up "jackrabbit land," bring groves. Whole communities grew up in Southern California under the impetus of this sort of promotional appeal.* Some of these communities, such as San Bernardino, Redlands and Riverside became full-fledged cities.

---

*In Leland Cooley's historical novel, *California,* to be published in September 1973, the result and the evolution of these land promotions is fully and excitingly told.

Now, a century later, huge development corporations, foremost among them Kaiser-Aetna, have revived and refined the plan in their "Rancho California" and "The Groves" developments in Southern California. Thousands of acres of what was once Mexican-American *rancho* land have been subdivided into small agricultural parcels, fully developed with paved streets, curbs, underground utilities, drains and on-site irrigation systems and set out in a great variety of "orchardettes."

The most popular crops are oranges, lemons and avocados. Several developers in northern California also plan to parcel up vineyards and Bartlett-pear, cherry and English-walnut orchards. In Florida, the crops are citrus, avocado and papaya.

Typical of sound planning and development in this new "minifarm" concept is Kaiser-Aetna's The Groves, south of Santa Barbara and Ventura and adjacent to Camarillo, California. The developer calls the new 10,000-acre gentleman farmers' community "Amberton." Less than a half hour's drive inland from the Pacific Coast, it lies in a verdant valley and reaches up along the gentle slopes of the surrounding coastal hills. The area has long been successful "avocado country."

Nearby, Amberton's "gentleman farmers" and their families can find almost every conceivable recreational option, with the exception of skiing. And the climate is representative of Southern California's best. Advertising aside, those are well-established facts.

Another well-established fact—the first two units of The Groves are sold out. Each parcel, ranging in size from 2-plus to 25-plus acres is fully planted with young avocado trees. As of January 1, 1973, they were doing so well that company agricultural officials expect the trees to begin bearing some fruit from one to two seasons earlier than usual.

By the time this book reaches your bookstore, Grove III will be ready for sale. Since the orientation of the third unit is more toward residential sites, many of the plots are smaller, from fully improved one-acre sites at about $14,000 to a fully improved three-acre "orchardette" at approximately $30,000.

We visited The Groves and received a very interesting lesson in the economics of avocado raising from Don Scanlin, Kaiser-Aetna's project manager. Later, we were updated by Jim Tyner of the sales department.

A new "gentleman grower" will find that the developer has paved all of the streets and dedicated them to Ventura County without assessment to the new owners. The developer has also put utilities underground (water, telephone, electricity and natural gas) and has built in the latest scientific drip method of irrigation to each parcel. The revolutionary system was devised and proved in Israel and brought here by Kaiser-Aetna.

The new owners will find that the developer has planted 120 healthy avocado trees to the acre and will provide a highly professional farm-management service that will take care of absolutely everything but the harvesting of the fruit for around $260 per acre per year. This includes the cost of irrigation water, fertilizer, pruning, intercropping and tilling. Harvesting by Calavo or one of the smaller co-ops costs about a penny a pound. For the past five years, the price in the orchard has been conservatively estimated at 25 cents a pound.

Under *optimum* conditions, mature trees will produce about 12,000 pounds of avocados per acre which translates into a *gross income* of around $3,000 an acre at the 25 cents per pound price.

How soon can an owner expect to receive some income from the trees? None for the first three years; however, there could be some very valuable tax write-offs.

Using an earlier *ultraconservative* estimate of 15 cents per pound projected price, and assuming normal conditions, *gross income per acre* might approximate these figures:

AGE OF TREE IN YEARS	FORTY POUND BOXES PER TREE	ESTIMATED DOLLAR INCOME PER ACRE
1	0	0
2	0	0
3	.25	0
4	.50	180
5	1.0	360
6	1.5	540
7	2.0	720
8	3.0	1,080
9	4.0	1,400
10 (Mature)	5.0 (Mature)	1,800 (Mature)

Beginning at the fourth year, the avocado trees may be depreciated over a thirty-five-year period. The irrigation system may be depreciated over ten years. We were also told that in certain situations accelerated depreciation schedules may apply. But the company goes to great pains in its literature and in conversations to make clear a prospective buyer's need to discuss these matters in detail with the family tax consultant. It also enumerates a number of conditions that may adversely affect a crop. After reading them, one concludes that while avocados are not "fragile," they may be "susceptible." And the same may be said for citrus trees.

So if Mother Nature cooperates, if the market holds, and if all of the projections prove accurate, it is possible for a modestly set-up "gentleman orchardist" to pay a substantial amount toward the purchase and maintenance of such a place without diverting critical sums from other income. At worst, one can wind up living in a pleasant low-density semi-rural development and have a lot of avocado salads and cocktail dip.

In the case of Kaiser-Aetna's agricultural developments, it would seem that the projections have been done with the same care used in making projections for their own commercial agricultural enterprises, which comprise some of the most successful in the country. As one owner at The Groves said, "If you can't partner with them, you can't partner with anybody."

What we said earlier about the "gamble" in farming holds true in any kind of agricultural endeavor, so one should be prepared to accept the entire expense if an act of God ruins a crop in his general locality.

Incidentally, the current (1973) property tax rate at Amberton is $9.23 per $100, which means that a $25,000 grove would pay $480.75 a year in taxes. That figure would increase accordingly if a residence were built.

One may purchase in The Groves under a variety of options. The simplest formula requires 15 percent down, plus one year of prepaid interest computed at 7-3/4 percent per annum. It is said that this prepaid interest formula is designed to give the buyer an added tax advantage. That would depend upon individual circumstances.

We repeat again: In choosing a particular development to describe, we are not implying that it is the only good one. In this instance, The Groves was chosen as being a typical example of careful planning and reasonable performance within its category.

After talking with a number of developers from coast to coast it seems we may expect many variations on this "gentleman farmer" theme. Soon a family will be able to raise pecans in Georgia, limes in Florida, pineapples in Hawaii, artichokes in California, peanuts in Alabama, and heaven only knows what else on his own "place." Ag-management firms will do all of the dirty work for a fixed fee and co-ops will take care of harvesting, packing and marketing—also for a fee. All an owner will need is sufficient financial resources to carry his end of the bargain in case things do not always meet expectations. This means income enough to live in the manner to which the family has become accustomed while paying principal, interest, taxes and maintenance on buildings, and the contracted price required by the ag-management group for doing everything necessary to insure a healthy grove.

There is such a thing as crop insurance for the big operators, but it is hardly worthwhile for a two-acre place. So the gentleman farmer and his family had better do whatever possible to propitiate the Gods of Wind, Rain, Earthquake, Freeze, Drought and Blight; for in the end, these are the misfortunes that could, but probably will not, send him down to the saloon to commiserate with the commercial "big boys" who got clobbered too. However, nature has provided a sort of built-in insurance by suiting the fruit to the climate. The possibility of catastrophic extremes is regarded as remote.

All told though, as one of the locals put it, "It's a fine way of life fer them as can git it to do."

32. *One of a score of new residences being built at The Groves by owners of the "pre-fab" farms. Most residences are in the $40,000 and up class . . . exclusive of trees, irrigation, and basic utilities. Other, more modest preplanted groves are planned in subsequent units of the 10,000-acre development. In nearby Camarillo, "gentlepeople" farmers will find complete shopping services. Los Angeles is an easy hour's freeway drive. It is a 20-minute drive to excellent beaches.*

33. *Several hundred acres of "pre-fab" orchards or groves are visible here. Water tank in distance provides pressure for innovative irrigation system that was tested in Israel and brought to The Groves by Kaiser-Aetna. In five years or less, this rolling hill country will be a "forest" of semi-tropical avocado trees, hopefully laden with highly marketable fruit.*

34. *Display home at The Groves in background; new residence being constructed by owner in middle distance. Each "farm" or "orchard" ranges in size from 2-plus to 25-plus acres, fully planted with healthy young avocado trees. See Chapter 13 for some interesting economic details and profit projections.*

35. *The model or "display home" built by Kaiser-Aetna at its "pre-fab farm" development, The Groves, at Amberton near Oxnard, California. This is famous citrus and avocado country.*

14.
The New "Communes"

The Greeks had a word for it; the Romans borrowed it; and about seven years ago major developers began adopting it, with variations, in the United States and in a number of foreign countries. The word was *condominium*—probably the least lovely and most unwieldy word in real estate jargon. A loose conjunction of two Latin words, *communis* (community) and *dominium* (dominion), it identifies a residential or business property owned jointly by a number of persons who have a fee simple "dominion" over their portion of the project. In addition they own, in common, an undivided share in the facilities and grounds.

There are sophisticated variations of the basic condominium concept. They seem to be limited only by the imagination, ingenuity and legal virtuosity of the developing organizations.

The condominium idea has a number of advantages, both for the developer and for the owner. It is not within the purview of this book to explore the manifold financing techniques that make the idea appealing to developers and their backers. For the time being, suffice it to say that in many instances—

especially where the condominiums are presold before they are actually built, or during the time they are being built—the developer has a very real leverage advantage.

In its simplest form, a developer gains leverage by acquiring a property or initiating a project with the smallest possible investment of his own, or borrowed money, sells the property before it is fully paid out, and pockets his profit. (The same principle works for the *investor* who buys with a low down payment and sells for a profit before the property is paid out.)

There is another advantage for the developer. Where zoning permits the higher density usually required for this version of the multiple dwelling, many more units can be concentrated on a given parcel of land than are possible under the "home-and-lot" concept. With land costs following suit, the condominium concept may allow the developer to give more living space for the price than his "single-family detached dwelling" competitor.

The condominium may be a primary home in a suburb or it may be a second-home recreational dwelling. It also may be part of a rental management pool in which the owner "joins" (for a fee) an organization that undertakes to rent out his second-home condominium for a portion of the most desirable seasons. Under such a plan the rental management organization may take as much as 20 percent commission for its services. The owner of the condominium may be told he can expect as much as 10 percent gross return on his investment from which, under certain circumstances, he may be able to deduct substantial sums for maintenance and depreciation from his federal and state income taxes.

Any prospective condominium buyer who is seeking both a part-time recreational residence and a *tax shelter* had better have a heart-to-heart talk with a good tax consultant, and with the Internal Revenue Service.

Hard-pressed to keep up with the innovations being conceived by developers and their tax lawyers, the IRS could be tempted to cover many situations under one blanket. There have been so many varied requests that the IRS is asking some owners to sign a waiver of the three-year statute of limitations. The waiver gives the IRS five years to sort out and adjudicate an exemption claim before the limitation runs out.

Moreover, where rental management agreements are a part of the deal, even though they are optional, the Securities and Exchange Commission is now getting involved. The government's contention is that a condominium owner who invests primarily for the purpose of realizing a profit or a "dividend" is, in fact, buying a "security" and as such the deal should come under the SEC.

A few years ago the mere idea of having to deal with both the IRS and the SEC sent developers and their bankers into "conniption fits." When several large developers—including the Maui Hilton in Hawaii—decided the lesser of two evils would be the registration of their offerings with the SEC, a precedent may have been set.

From the developers' point of view the SEC registration has two distinct disadvantages: It takes months to process a registration and it can add upward of $1,000 to the cost of a unit, thereby depriving the project of a considerable competitive advantage. Also, there is a question as to whether or not the salesmen offering the deals are real estate salesmen, qualified as such, or securities brokers who should be qualified—or both.

Some developers are suggesting that the whole jurisdiction be embraced by a new arm of HUD set up under new regulations acceptable to both the IRS and the SEC. And just as many, perhaps more, are crying, "For God's sake, don't encourage still another layer of federal bureaucracy!"

After talking with the IRS, it seems clear that the "Service" is not going to look kindly on any device that results in a lowering of its gross "take" from property income without making up the difference with some very creative new interpretations. In short, " . . . a tax by any other name will be just as painful."

Technical disadvantages aside, there is much to be said for the condominium concept as a primary residence and as a second home. In well-chosen, carefully developed locations, the majority of condominiums have shown substantial gains in value. This has been particularly true in the popular all-year recreational areas.

Units in U.S. Plywood's *Crystal Shores* condominium development on the lakefront at Incline Village, Lake Tahoe—a pioneer Nevada project—have doubled in price since their opening in the mid-1960s. So have the *Tahoe City* condominiums on the California side; and the same is true of a dozen such developments in Miami, Fort Lauderdale, Hollywood, Fort Myers and Tampa, Florida. And it will undoubtedly be true in the greater Orlando area under the phenomenal impetus imparted to that entire region by Disney World and by the other "theme parks" and recreational complexes that are moving into the shelter of the giant Disney shadow.

The old bromide that successful real estate investment depends upon three things—location, location and location—is an amusing oversimplification. To location must be added timing, quality and price.

Some sales analysis will tell you that it matters little *when* you buy and at *what price,* so long as location and the other factors are right—that values are certain to soar. In a very general way that is true. And still we can cite instance after instance where location and timing seemed to be "right on" but where quality (design concept and execution) and price were out of kilter with the market. At Lake Tahoe's *Incline Village,* a well-designed high-rise condominium called *Crystal Towers* sold out immediately while a medium-sized "row house" condominium in the same general area still had units for sale three years after the "grand opening." To many prospects, both interior and exterior design was questionable and so were the price and the maintenance charges.

It seems reasonable to expect, however, that values, in general, will rise substantially as land use restrictions limit the amount of new residential construction around the seventy-mile shoreline of the High Sierra lake. In the case of the overpriced development, values will catch up with price, design notwithstanding. Here again the law of supply and demand will determine the market.

At Tahoe, as in other localities where conservationists are squared off with developers, the vacant-property owner finds himself on the horns of a dilemma; he may not be able to use his property as he had planned; but, on the other hand, the restrictions imposed by the conservationist-inspired regulations may end up increasing land values. (And it is fair to say that ecological "overkill" may render some land unsalable, too.)

If a family is hung up on the traditional concept of ownership ("We want a *particular* piece of land that we can call our own and we want our own house on it"), then the condominium may present some philosophical problems. If a small family is willing to weigh economical and recreational advantages against the traditional "man's home is his castle" attitude; if the family can settle for the development's clubhouse and "fun-in-the-sun" facilities; if it can live with its small walled-in patio as against the old spacious fenced-in family backyard—then the condominium can be a satisfying investment, particularly if value is reckoned in both pleasure and profit.

Among the variations on the condominium primary-and-second-home theme is that offered by an Illinois developer, the Leisure Technology Corporation.

LTC's "new wrinkle" is the purchase of a primary-home condominium at its Cambridge-on-the-Lake project in Buffalo Grove, Illinois, plus a six-way joint ownership in a condominium at the developer's Seven Lakes project in Fort Myers, Florida.

What this means, apparently, is joint ownership with five other parties in a condominium dwelling that will be shared as a recreational second home. A family takes a full-time primary residence condominium at Cambridge-on-the-Lake in Illinois and, by a mutually agreed-upon plan, may spend up to two months (one-sixth of the year) in residence at the *shared ownership* facility in Florida.

This seems to have been the forerunner of a still more sophisticated concept that is gaining in popularity at ski resorts and in Hawaii and Florida too. It is called the "TSO Plan."

TSO stands for Time Shared Ownership, and the term is explicit. A number of owners, not necessarily known to one another, buy a pro rata use of a vacation condominium. The developer sets up a management company. An annual fee is computed that includes the cost of the furniture, bedding, dishes, utensils, cleaning, repairs, replacements—the works. As one developer put it, "All a Time Share Owner needs to bring is himself, his toothbrush and his booze."

In order to determine costs on this new investment concept, we went to the pioneer developer, The Warner-National Corporation, Cincinnati, Ohio. Warner-National is the owner of an unusual spa development on the California side of Lake Tahoe.

Brockway Springs is a complete modern "revival" of what was once the most prestigious summer resort on the famous lake. But time took its toll, and as the founding members passed away, the resort fell into disrepair. Later, a fire finished the sad story.

Starting from scratch—and using the renowned hot mineral springs as a focal point—the new developer is creating a modern year-round spa in what is surely a mountain lake setting surpassed by few places in the world. The Innisfree Corporation, a wholly owned subsidiary of Hyatt House, acts as sales and operations representative on the project. Not all of their condominium units are on a Time Shared Ownership basis.

To give the reader some idea of price ranges in a top quality TSO project, we asked for some general information that applied as of January 1, 1973. It follows, in simplified form:

At Brockway Springs, TSO condominiums range in size from one to four bedrooms. Each TSO owner holds a one-eleventh undivided interest in the unit of his choice. This entitles the owner's family (or friends) to use the unit for two two-week periods during the occupancy year. (Management holds the units vacant for two weeks each year for cleaning and refurbishing—"off season," of course.)

The cost of the occupancy depends upon the time of year the owners wish to use the two two-week periods. Costs are highest during the midsummer vacation and midwinter skiing seasons, more reasonable during the adjacent two-week periods on either side of those prime summer-winter periods, most reasonable during the spring and fall "off seasons." The TSO year begins on the second Friday in January of each year.

Using a two-bedroom TSO unit as an average example, we find that the cost of the one-eleventh ownership in peak periods is $8,500; a two-week summer period is $5,000; and the peak winter occupancy period (excluding December 14 to January 10 which costs $9,000) is $3,500. To all TSO purchase prices must be added a pro rata share of annual maintenance costs plus a one-eleventh share of the total furniture package on the unit.

To quote the extremes, a one-bedroom TSO unit purchased for the least desirable two-week periods could cost as little as $4,000, while a four-bedroom luxury unit bought for use during the peak seasonal periods could cost as much as $27,000.

Using the two-bedroom unit as an average again, the condominium fee, property taxes, furniture replacement costs, housekeeping fees (including linen service, general maintenance and repair costs), insurance and utilities, will run $453 a year or $38 a month.

By contrast, the one-bedroom unit would cost $409 a year and the four-bedroom apartment would cost $650 a year. Since these monthly charges include just about everything a home owner could possibly need in terms of facilities and services, they seem moderate when compared to the cost of maintaining on an annual basis a second home used only a few weeks in a year.

At first blush the TSO idea may seem like another gimmick, but after as thorough an analysis of the plan as is possible so early in its practice in the United States, we feel that it might well be a sound investment for an active young family in need of an inexpensive second-home recreational dwelling. This would be particularly true if the young family had already committed itself to a mortgage on a primary residence.

If we compare the TSO purchase price against a two-week summer rental and a two-week winter rental for a family of four, a moderately priced TSO makes more sense.

Using average two-bedroom rentals in two diversified all-year resort areas as the basis for computations, a family of four would expect to spend around $1,200 for shelter for two two-week periods.

Assuming that inflation did not increase those rental rates drastically, in seven years the family would have spent $10,500 for vacation shelter.

The same family could have purchased a TSO condominium for around $10,000, and at the end of the seventh year they would be "home free" to all intents and purposes. True, the note runs for ten years, but by the seventh year the principal is being amortized very quickly. Moreover, they have had the advantage of interest and tax deductions on their purchase, an "edge" they do not enjoy as renters. And, if they have chosen a well-conceived TSO in a fine resort area, they will undoubtedly have realized a potential profit on the value of their one-eleventh ownership share.

The assumption that resort rentals would not increase drastically is not realistic, based on past history and expert projections for the future. So, in the event such rental inflation does take place, the argument in favor of the TSO gets even better since the trust deed and note is reckoned at the then existing value of the dollar, not on some inflation value projected into the future. The only place that inflation will probably be reflected in a TSO purchase is in the owner's share of the annual service and maintenance fee which, even if it doubled in ten years, would still be relatively nominal.

There is, of course, another advantage to the TSO concept. If the share-owner family finds it will not be using the unit for one of the two-week periods, it may be leased to friends or family. Even at very competitive prices, the rental will more than cover the owner's share of the annual upkeep. And, too, there may be another advantage. Although developers' representatives would not commit themselves, a possibility exists that the owner could take some tax depreciation on the rented unit, thereby "sweetening" the deal accordingly.

Time Shared Ownership is an interesting idea that should prove even more successful here than it has been in European ski resorts.

36. Lodge condominiums at Sunriver, shown here, have a bath and fire-place for each bedroom. The two-bedroom condominiums can be converted into hotel accommodations, one with kitchen, dining, and living rooms. Each accommodation has a private entrance and private patio deck.

37. Snowbird Village and lower tram station. In the famous Wasatch Range and not far from the internationally known resort, Alta, this spectacular new all-year resort is already enjoying phenomenal popularity. Garaventa of Switzerland engineered the Snowbird Tram, one of the largest in the world. From an 8,100-foot base elevation it rises to the 11,000-foot summit of Hidden Peak, carrying 125 passengers per cabin. The 2,900-foot vertical rise takes approximately 6 minutes. Four double-passenger chair lifts presently serve the area's runs that offer everything, from beginner to expert trails. Excellent snow may be found from November to May.

38. Snowbird, Utah. "Turramurra," the exciting new all-year resort's newest condominium/hotel complex, opened in the winter of '73. It's amenities are obvious in this architects' rendition. The spectacular location is a scant 45 minutes from downtown Salt Lake City.

39. An outstanding example of good design and land use. These condominiums at Northstar—at Tahoe—have been built to "blend" into the surrounding terrain and forest. An absolute minimum of trees were disturbed and, during construction, heavy plank guards were wired around trunks to avoid skinning by heavy equipment. Natural stream banks were carefully preserved.

At the end of 1972, 242 condominiums were under construction. Two hundred seventy-one more are scheduled for 1973. Nowhere did construction intrude on the surrounding natural terrain. [Photograph by Chapman Wentworth, Incline Village, Nevada.]

40. The slopes at Northstar, developed by Trimont Land Company, a division of Fibreboard Corporation, on Highway 267, seven miles north of Lake Tahoe between Kings Beach and Truckee. This aerial photo looks west, with Squaw Peak at top center. Mount Pluto is in middistance, upper left. Five double-chair lifts and ten miles of superb trails tempted 3,000 skiers, a capacity crowd, in less than a week after opening during the 1972 holiday season.

The public is welcome in this private second-home recreational development until the 3,000 skier cut-off point is reached . . . a unique plan that guarantees owners and early birds alike a chance at uncrowded slopes and lifts. [Photograph by Chapman Wentworth, Incline Village, Nevada.]

41. *Bit Springs Inn at Incline Village, Lake Tahoe, is one of several ski facilities under construction at Northstar where vacationers may buy or rent equipment, warm themselves and "recharge" their energy reserves for another go at the 10 miles of slopes.*

Within easy driving distance are Squaw Valley and Ski Incline. [Photograph by Holly Wilson, Wentworth & Associates.]

42. *Ski Hill Grooming: Photograph above is a part of Northstar at Tahoe's large fleet of snow-grooming machines. The new resort, 7 miles north of Lake Tahoe, has enough equipment to pack all runs daily. Equipment such as this has brought on the boom of skiing, which is no longer a sport only for athletes. [Photograph courtesy of Wentworth & Associates.]*

15.
Our New "Mobile" Life-Style

In years gone by anyone undertaking a book on land investment would have passed over the real estate developments catering to those Americans who had chosen to live in so-called mobile home parks. Spaces were rented, not sold, and the residents were usually older couples who no longer wanted the expense and responsibility of a large house, preferring to live with congenial peers close by a place where the fishing or the golf or the "settin' an' rockin' " were good. But mostly, they wanted to be where the "weather was good." As a consequence, the first of these places began to spring up in Florida and elsewhere along the South Atlantic and the Gulf Coast; in California and in Baja California, principally at a lovely spot of sandy shoreline called Estero Beach, south of Ensenada.

As the mobile home manufacturers began to be more certain of their market, their product improved and became far more sophisticated both in construction and styling. By the early 1960s, many of the better mobile homes were rivaling conventional on-site construction in square footage, in excellence of design and in other esthetic considerations. And they enjoyed another advantage: they were prefabricated and hauled to their location for final assembly. What this new technology achieved was a home comparable in most respects to a conventional dwelling of the same size but selling, complete, for thousands of dollars less.

The economic appeal and the ease of upkeep were irresistible to older couples. Very soon the primitive "trailer parks" with publicly shared toilets and inadequate laundry facilities began to evolve into minisuburbs complete with streets, sidewalks, parks, underground utilities and on-site sewer connections.

In addition, the developers provided clubhouses, putting courses, shuffleboard courts, laundry rooms, community garden space and many other amenities. For those attuned to "tin-box living," as one dour real estate writer termed it, the mobile home park made possible a most agreeable new life-style. For several million American couples, it still is.

It was from these early "total living" mobile home parks that the large tract developers borrowed many of their suburban innovations. In recent years these have now been elaborated by developers to the point where the mobile home community seems to have become a microcosmic imitation when, in fact, the new total living suburban communities are a macrocosmic evolution.

There were, and still are, fine investment possibilities in the mobile homesite market. In the past, establishing mobile home communities was primarily for capital investments suitable only for developers with the know-how and financing. The individual who wished to purchase his own "pad" in a park found little opportunity to do so. Most mobile home parks were set up to produce space rental income, and this is still true today.

But now a few are beginning to sell the condominium idea—fee simple ownership of your own individual "lot" and an undivided ownership in all of the common facilities such as clubhouses, swimming pools, tennis courts, golf courses and all the rest. Some developers, finding a nice source of profit in the recreation facilities, retain ownership of them and charge a monthly fee for their use.

These new "condo-parks" may be found in virtually every state in the union now, and the best of them seemed to offer really excellent investment possibilities for the individual owner. But it is important to understand that, unlike the well-located, well-planned conventional residential investment in which both dwelling and the land it stands on increase in value, a person buying into a mobile home park of comparable quality will find that the largest increase in value will come from the land itself.

Several weeks before this book was written, the authors visited mobile home parks for a three-week period. These forty-two parks were located in five states from Oregon to Florida. All sold lots on the fee-simple cooperative or condominium plan. All had been established for at least four years. The three oldest parks had been established in 1963 and 1964. Since in all but the most "posh" second-home parks, the economics of the industry tend to make them competitive and therefore comparable, the information gained represented a fair average experience.

Boiled down to the absolute essential conclusion, the figures show that while mobile homes depreciate much faster than a conventional residence of the same square footage, the increase in value of the fee-simple land in a well-operated park more than offset the decrease in value of the dwelling.

On resales, a number of owners were able to show a substantial profit, not only on the mobile "coach" lot but also on the coach itself. In most instances the profit included the extras the owners had put in; rain gutters, drains, skirting around the bottom of the vehicles (in most states they are taxed as such), cement block planters, rock lawns, awnings, car ports, ramadas, aluminum garden tool sheds, fencing and other "fancying up."

Some investment-minded owners had seen the possibilities and had purchased several choice lots early in the offering. In more than one instance, we found owners who had realized enough net profit on their early mobile homes to buy much more modern coaches and locate them on the speculative lots.

In all but the newest parks surveyed, there were no vacant company lots for sale. And there were few resales posted on the board provided for that purpose in the clubhouses. Management told us that the popularity of these better located and better designed parks is such that the developers are now limiting the number of fee-simple lots at one to a customer. However, most developers give the original owners an option to buy at a predevelopment price in the extensions or new units planned adjacent to the original installations.

"Even though we do not make a profit from the installation of the coaches themselves, we do not want a checkerboard situation—vacant speculation lots scattered through the development," said one developer. "Psychologically it's very poor. And economically too; because a potential buyer looking in figures the place isn't going so well. We tell our original owners that it really works against them too."

In one ten-year-old park near San Diego, California, containing 360 "spaces" averaging about 50 x 75 feet, we counted only six vacant lots. Four were resales from which the original mobile homes had been removed. Four new mobile homes were being installed by owners who had sold their older coaches.

The depreciation figures were interesting:

> 20% the first year
> 10% the second year
> 10% the third year
> 10% the fourth year
> 5% each year thereafter.*

A ten-year-old 10 x 50 feet two-bedroom coach, for which the owners had paid $6,000 and had put in roughly $2,000 worth of "improvements," had depreciated to approximately $3,600. But they had been able to sell it for $4,000 to a couple who wanted to move it to a second-home location near Palm Springs, California.

"Even though we're putting a larger, more modern coach on the same lot, we were able to keep most of the landscaping. We

---

*One mobile-home dealer cut those depreciation figures in half, "on the newest 'double' models."

don't think it's 'sharp' bookkeeping to add what it would cost us to replace the plants and things to the *profit* we figured we made. Do you?" they asked.

When we agreed that it was reasonable, by their figuring, the man and his wife estimated that, time (and pleasure) aside, they had put close to $800 in landscaping and citrus trees, the latter bearing profusely.

Reckoned on those figures, they made a $1,200 profit on the transaction—enough to offset the 10 percent down payment on the new mobile home. Amortizing the $4,000 they were out-of-pocket over ten years means that the couple paid only $400 a year for basic shelter. Add to that the $300 annual charge ($25 monthly) for water, gas, club facilities and public area maintenance, shelter and recreation cost them $700 a year or approximately $58 a month. Even when they added insurance, vehicle license taxes, gas for cooking and heating, the retired couple still reckoned their gross monthly living cost, less food, medical and transportation, at under $70 a month.

There have been a number of comparative studies that measured the mobile home investment against a conventional home of the same approximate size. These studies have, until recently, compared "apples and oranges" in that they assumed the mobile home would stand on a rental site in which the owner gained no equity, while the conventional dwelling was an essential part of the land it stands on and therefore increased in value as land values increased.

Using that yardstick, the Federal Reserve Bank of Boston concluded in a 1970 study that in terms of *owned assets* the case was markedly better for the owner of a conventional residence. Conversely, the mobile home owner enjoyed a much lower monthly outlay for the same square footage of living space.

Under the new condominium concept of mobile park development, the mobile home owners may gain *both* advantages.

Some idea of what can happen to values in nine years may be had by comparing the basic deal offered by the San Luis Rey Mobile Home Park just a stone's throw from the historic San Luis Rey Mission in Southern California.

A brochure secured from the developer in 1964 offered the following inducements:

YOUR CLUBHOUSE & RECREATION AREA

ACTUAL PHOTO

OWN YOUR OWN MOBILE HOME ESTATE

* MINIMUM SIZE: Lots 40' x 60' — Mobile Homes 10' x 40'.
* CITY Water, City Sewer, Natural Gas, Underground 120-V - 240-V, Piped in TV, Club House, Restaurant Facilities.
* COMPLETE RECREATIONAL Facilities, including 40' Fishing & Pleasure Boat, now moored at the Oceanside Small Craft Harbor. 9-Hole Putting Green.
* YOU OWN an individual interest in the entire park and all its assets . . . in addition to owning your own lot.
* YOU GET a policy of title insurance from T.I.&T. Co., the world's largest.

AFTER PURCHASE FOR AS LITTLE AS $9.00 Per Month

All of the above fabulous living can be yours — the $9.00 per month pays: *your water bill — *your real estate property taxes — *ownership in all of the above facilities with full time management. No children. No pets.

DON'T CONFUSE OUR PARK WITH THE ONE IN FRONT OF THE MISSION

4202 Mission Ave. (Hwy. 76) Oceanside

LOOK FOR THE SIGN WITH THE WORDS

"OWN YOUR OWN"

SHOW SPECIAL

OUR PACKAGE DEAL

All the Benefits Listed on This Circular — Plus a 12' x 55' - 1 or 2-Bedroom Mobile Home. Completely Furnished, Ready to Live In.

For Only

$9,000

Includes HOME and LOT

AS LOW AS **10%** DOWN

THIS OFFER LIMITED

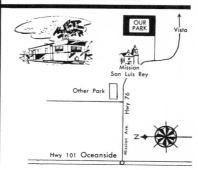

On January 8, 1973, we revisited the park. Its 300 spaces had been sold out for several years, mostly to retirees. In a tour through the streets we found only two spaces that seemed to have been left vacant for some time. Several others—resales, we were told—had elaborate new mobile homes in the course of installation. The entire park had the look of solid development. The residents we chatted with at the excellent community clubhouse were all unequivocal "rooters" for the San Luis Rey life-style.

From them we learned that no resident in the park looked forward to less than double his lot investment in the event of a resale. They acknowledged that the depreciation was in the coach. On the bulletin board in the clubhouse there was ample evidence that the estimate was not overly optimistic. The lot value? From fee-simple lots that averaged in size from the 40 x 60 foot minimum (advertised in the pamphlet) to 50 x 61-plus foot lots, resale prices ranged from $12,000 to $18,000, complete with mobile home. Originally the lots were priced from $3,500 to $7,500.

It seems then that the formula—*increased land values "wash out" coach depreciation*—is generally true. Then too, one can reckon some of the profit in the enjoyment, convenience, economy and security of living in such a community.

This older mobile home park was used as an example because we were able to follow the "owner experience" over a long period of time. We might just as well have used Art Linkletter's remarkable Sierra Dawn development near Hemet, California, for it had impressed us as an excellent investment possibility when we visited it in 1965 while researching our first book on retirement. For that matter, we might also have used the mobile parks developed by "Maestro" Lawrence Welk or by actor Fess Parker. The only disadvantage in using one of the glamour show business "name" parks is that they do enjoy a special merchandising "edge" that enhances their investment desirability over lesser-known competition.

One of the trouble areas a potential mobile home park resident owner must think about is zoning. Many of the parks are located in outlying areas which have not been finally zoned. It is very important to know *who and what* your "development neighbors" will be.

We know of two parks that were "out in the country" when they were approved. Today one of those parks shares a common property line with a two-stage sewage treatment plant that can, on occasion, "stink to high heaven"—and the park is downwind of it! The plant was located there to serve a half dozen new housing developments that sprang up later on what was once a very productive commercial vegetable farm in a verdant valley.

In the second case a large cabinet shop providing kitchen and bathroom units for tract house builders was constructed later just across the fence from the mobile home park. Planers and routers scream through wood from eight in the morning until four-thirty in the afternoon, six days a week. And a burner showers ash and sometimes live sparks over the entire area.

There is no guarantee that the zoning prevalent when a buyer makes his decision will hold indefinitely. So it is wise to question very closely what changes are apt to be made. That is best done by going to county planning offices and also by making discreet inquiries at the local utility companies. It is also worth going to the county assessor's office to check the nature and direction of past growth. Armed with this information, it is possible to project the sort of surrounding development one is likely to have in years to come.

Some mobile home parks have actually been harbingers of conventional residential development. With more attention being paid now to the design of tracts, it is less likely that they will detract from a pleasing area. In many cases, because of the several advantages still enjoyed by mobile home owners, new tracts may actually enhance property values.

One good thing to keep in mind: As so-called mobile homes become larger, more sophisticated in design and stronger in construction, they also become more vulnerable to the pressures brought by competitive home developers, and owners, too, who are jealous of the several real advantages enjoyed by the M.H. buffs, not the least of which are the low cost per square foot of finished living space, lower upkeep and lower taxes.

One way to avoid most of these problems is to make your purchase in one of the new omnibus communities that includes a special section set aside and designed for those who prefer to live in a mobile home. You may pay a bit more for your lot. But you may get a lot more for your money in peripheral advantages, including the use of top-quality recreational facilities. The zoning worry is done away with. The question of vehicle-license tax versus residential tax will probably not be resolved in most states for many years. In any case, you will have to pay a property tax on the land itself. And, as of now, those taxes are really minimal.

In short, as with any other major personal investment in living space, it is necessary to investigate before you invest.

43. *There are two Olympic-size swimming pools at Outdoor Resorts of America's Nettles Island complex. In addition to the pools and watersports on the colorful Indian River—a fisherman's paradise—the vast resort complex features a large recreational area with full facilities for tennis, miniature golf, shuffleboard, volleyball, and horseshoes, plus a recreational lodge and children's playground. Attractively landscaped recreational vehicle sites number 1585, all equipped with 5-point hookups. More than 350 of the sites are on the waterfront. For fine dining and quality nightly entertainment, guests have easy access to the new Sheraton Resort Inn, situated conveniently within the complex. The Nettles Island resort is located on Highway A1A on the Atlantic Ocean, near Stuart, Florida. [Photograph, courtesy of the Russell Ray Studios, Nashville, Tennessee.]*

44. A nine hole chip-'n'-putt golf course and beautiful Lake Davenport are two of the major recreational features at Outdoors Resorts of America at Orlando/Disney World. Other attractions include an Olympic-size swimming pool, tennis and shuffleboard courts, miniature golf, and a two-story recreation lodge. All of this—only five miles from the entrance to Disney World—makes Outdoor Resorts a prime example of the advantages of location in good development. [Photograph, courtesy of Russell Ray Studios, Nashville, Tennessee.]

45. *Boating, fishing, scuba diving and skiing are all in the day's fun for recreational vehicle campers at Outdoor Resorts of America at Nettles Island. This 130-acre resort complex near Stuart, Florida, has an ocean beach and an island in the Indian River. There are 1,585 recreational vehicle sites including 360 waterfront lots. Recreational facilities include two Olympic-size pools, a recreation lodge, tennis and shuffleboard courts, miniature golf and areas for a variety of other games and sports.*

Paved drives, concrete patios with picnic tables, landscaped sites, and full utility hookups are all standard at any Outdoor Resorts of America's recreational vehicle resorts.

16.
Raw Land

In the original and revised editions of *The Simple Truth about Western Land Investment,* the main thrust of our study was concerned with "inexpensive land in the path of progress."

In a sense now, almost all of our habitable land is in the path of progress. Millions of acres of "raw" land—desert "jackrabbit land," scrub forest land, wooded land and remote coastal land— are still available in the path of, or astride, the ever probing tentacles of the "megaloctopus" that is every major urban and suburban population center in the Western world.

Now, when we revisit the open areas of ten years ago, we find new suburban cities. That is true along the entire eastern corridor, in Florida, along the Gulf Coast; and it is true in the areas surrounding Mobile, Atlanta, Birmingham and New Orleans; Chicago, Pittsburgh, Kansas City and St. Louis; and Dallas to Fort Worth, among others.

It is hard to believe our eyes as we travel south into Virginia and see what has happened from Fairfax to Petersburg. Historic battlegrounds with names that shine throughout the pages of our history are being outflanked by strip cities as more and more urban dwellers desert "urban cores" for clean living space—and in so doing bring with them most of the problems they are fleeing.

Price a piece of land along any of the main traffic routes and you'll get a graphic lesson in the real meaning of the law of supply and demand. (If you haven't already learned the lesson at your local supermarket!)

The strip-city principle first enunciated in our early land books still applies. In September of 1961, *U.S. News and World Report* published a map of United States strip cities. After securing permission we duplicated it with some additions supplied by our own research.

The magazine's pioneer study was extraordinarily accurate. It showed strip cities growing up between most of the major population centers along both coasts and between urban centers in our inland areas.

Today, our research shows that the marginal areas of twelve years ago are filled in solidly now. The strip city that reached from Seattle-Vancouver down to Eugene, Oregon, now extends with a few "gaps and detours" all the way south to San Francisco. There it merges with the strip city growing northward from San Diego and Los Angeles. Except for national and state parks, forest land and several huge military preserves, the entire Pacific Coast may be regarded as settled, although not always in classic urban patterns.

In earlier chapters on the land market and on the second-home recreational land boom, we have seen that no place is really remote anymore. Land promoters have invaded most *privately owned* open space. Some of the land they are peddling is so arid that the buzzards are on relief! But to hear them tell it on radio and TV, and in their expensive four-color brochures, even the most unanchored of these places is peripheral to paradise and within a "twenty-minute drive of beautiful downtown Somewhere." In most cases that would not be true unless your name were Foyt, Revson, Muther, Posey or Unser—and the "fuzz" was out to lunch!

True, it is still possible to drive "full bore" for three hours across an Indian reservation in Arizona or New Mexico without passing a community of any size. And Florida's Tamiami Trail could hardly be called "settled." But aside from specially preserved open spaces, usually under the jurisdiction of the federal and state governments, one seldom drives more than one hundred miles without coming to an important town or city.

The network of national and state roads in this country has been called "one of the miracles of our modern world." The accessibility such roads provide has much influence on present and future land values. It is along these good paved roads and within the rectangles of open country they enclose, that tomorrow's best land investment opportunities will be located.

Let's assume now that you have decided to invest in a parcel of "raw" land because it is still relatively inexpensive and because you feel that within five to ten years it will be located in a general area that seems certain to develop.

To begin with, if the land lies along one of the strip cities—let's say between Pittsburgh, Johnstown and Altoona, or between Raleigh and Atlanta—it already has some powerful influence at work on its value. But the simple presence of a piece of land in one of those growth areas does not guarantee that it will automatically be worth a lot more in the near future. There are two reasons:

First, the present owner, aware that he is in an area of activity, may be holding the price too high.

Second, a parcel might be worth a great deal less than a similar piece within a mile or so because of some peculiarity: lack of water, lack of good roads, lack of readily available utilities, type of soil, or poor topography and wrong zoning. Any one factor, or a combination of factors, may affect the land's value. Also, the use one intends to make of a piece of land, *and when*, has much to do with determining its eventual value; not to somebody else, but to you.

As we said earlier, the best way to sharpen one's foresight is to review one's hindsight, and it bears repeating. History is recorded hindsight. The local history of an area in which a person contemplates an investment in real estate is an accurate and open book, if one will take the time to do the research we have urged as absolutely necessary. You know why you want to invest. *The next thing is to price similar land in the area to make certain the parcel that interests you is fairly valued.* After that, check the zoning in the area. It may change over the years, but a change is not necessarily bad. In some instances, it could signal an overall value increase. There are scores of "hindsight" examples here in the United States and in Canada as well, where land use laws have changed under development pressure.

One of the most dramatic in recent times is the story (history) of the San Fernando Valley just over the Hollywood Hills from Los Angeles. NBC, Warner Brothers, Universal and Disney are there now. So are a thousand national and international corporations.

Budweiser not only brews its excellent product there but also, very effectively, competes with Disneyland, Knott's Berry Farm, Marineland and the Japanese Village and Deer Park by operating its own "Busch Gardens," a family amusement-park-zoo-museum, replete with everything from jungle boat rides to paper hankies to blot the foam from father's moustache.

Just under a half century ago, when the male half of this collaboration came down from his native city, San Francisco, he and his barefoot school chums used to hunt jackrabbits and rattlesnakes in the same general area. To the north, were alfalfa and wheat ranches. To the west, along what is now the Ventura Freeway, there were rich walnut and peach farms. And there were sleepy little towns with familiar names scattered along the broad, dusty valley—towns called North Hollywood, Sherman Oaks, Van Nuys, Girard, Tarzana (Edgar Rice Burroughs named it) and distant San Fernando, site of one of California's most famous missions and once the heart of a great grain-growing region.

Eight years later Victor Girard, who accurately described himself as a community builder, ran an ad in the *Los Angeles Times* that invited people to take a free bus ride from downtown Los Angeles to see his Walnut Acre Farms.

"Los Angeles is expanding directly toward Walnut Acre Farms," he wrote in his 1927 ad. "Ventura State Highway is crowded like a city street! Traffic increases each day. What was farmland a few years ago is now a thriving community. Land values are going up! They will continue to go up. Thousands of new people are pouring into Los Angeles each week. A new wave of real estate activity is starting. Prices are already headed for the apex! Visitors in Los Angeles are staying, are building homes. Walnut Acre Farms is strategically located to absorb the overflow. No one can predict what its value will be in two or three years—or even one year from now! Big profits for someone. Will you be the one? Investigate what a small investment in Walnut Acre Farms will do for you. Ask us. No obligations."

One Sunday our family put up a lunch and drove out over the narrow Cahuenga Pass road to the Ventura State Highway. There, in what is now the heart of a forest of high rise office buildings and a giant shopping complex, we found the first of the advertised land. The walnut trees, some mature and some just grafted and set out, were thriving in the clean air, brilliant sunshine and rich earth of the western San Fernando Valley. Years play tricks on memory, but we seem to remember a particularly fine five-acre parcel that could have been had for $2,000 with only 10 percent down. It was the opinion of the family elders that it was "a beautiful place all right, but much too far out. Los Angeles will grow down toward the beach and stop."

Three years ago we went to a party to celebrate the making of a new "millionairess." Her father and mother had bought twenty acres there. In time, the trees had gone but the land had been preserved in the estate. A family home had been built on one five-acre parcel. The fortunate lady who was our hostess had been born there. She had married in the early 1930s, and her new husband had given her a wedding present of two more acres—a bearing peach orchard—for which he paid $1,500 an acre.

In the mid-1930s business had grown up along the Ventura State Highway and the couple built a series of small stores that turned a comfortable profit, despite the depression. Then, after a long career in real estate, the husband died—too young, as so often happens—and the widow, in whose name most of the original property had been held, finally sold for $1,300,000. When last seen she was taking her daughter-in-law on a "Round-the-World" cruise while her son finished his overseas tour in the Marine Corps.

On a recent trip to Europe three of the passengers on a twelve-passenger French Line freighter were taking the first real holiday they had enjoyed in years. It was made possible by capital gains profits from land they had bought fifteen years earlier in what is now a suburb of Seattle, Washington.

A more recent example? In November of 1972, during a television promotion tour of our retirement book, *How to Avoid the Retirement Trap,* we stopped at a gas station at Winter Park, north of Orlando, Florida. Moments later a couple pulled up in a shiny new Mercedes-Benz 280 SE. It was so new it still bore the white oval European "ZED" plates. On the radiator grille it also displayed the small medallion that signified the owner had taken delivery on his car at Sindelfingen, the suburb of Stuttgart, Germany, where the factory is located.

Since ours bore that same medallion, as well as others from the countries we had driven in during a six months' research trip in 1969, a conversation ensued. We both agreed that we had bought excellent pieces of machinery and we both agreed they cost plenty! We said, "We've got to drive ours at least a hundred thousand miles · to make it pay out." The man laughed sympathetically.

"Disney bought me this car. And he's going to buy us a couple more like it when this wears out, if we don't wear out first!"

How had Disney bought this man his expensive foreign car? By choosing the Orlando area as the site of Disney World and sending real estate values skyrocketing for fifty miles around. When we explained our interest in land values, the couple—they have asked that we do not use their names—told us their story.

In 1942 the husband had been advised to move from Chicago because of the cold weather. With no experience except for a few years on a southern Illinois farm as a child, he and his wife "pulled up stakes" and bought an orange grove near Orlando.

Soon they signed a contract with a frozen concentrate corporation which took their entire crop. The contract became collateral for a bank loan with which they bought ten adjoining acres, making thirty acres in all.

"We sold out last year to a motel chain for $800,000," they said, "and you can bet that the only thing that hurt was the capital gains. Some of that land we bought for $600 an acre."

In September of 1972 while the press was preoccupied with presidential candidates, Sanford J. Ungar of the *Washington Post* filed a story to the *Los Angeles Times* in which it was revealed that Senator George McGovern had made substantial profits from a real estate investment in Maryland.

In 1966, according to the story, the presidential candidate had purchased thirteen acres for $12,000 from real estate speculators. Within two weeks, the story continued, George McGovern had sold off four acres to a surgeon for $26,000. He had more than doubled his money on less than one-third of the land—not an unusual happening. In fact, it is a classic example of how money is made in real estate by people with vision enough to see the possibilities of an area and who have persistence enough to *check the facts.*

Much more recently the press reported very respectable profits made by President Nixon from real estate purchased near the Florida White House.

When President Nixon chose San Clemente, California, as the site of his Western White House the effect on land values in the area was immediate. Surely, when the President of the United States moves in as a neighbor, regardless of the area, one could expect values to soar. But the underlying point is valid: if one knows in advance that a major development is about to take place in an area, the chances for a profitable investment are immeasureably enhanced.

Certainly, you will say, this is easier to accomplish in an area that clearly shows signs of growth. That is true. But it is also true that great fortunes have been made by some otherwise ordinary people who had the foresight to *buy* and *hold* in outlying areas where the possibility of growth was not so obvious, but where positive indicators could be found with some diligent digging.

Research may be more difficult where raw land is concerned. It is easy to become influenced or misled by promoters. Some raw-land-raw-deal operators will deliberately start a rumor about an area in which they wish to promote a deal. "We've got 'hard' information that a big new something-or-other is going in just below us." For diabolical creative larceny these questionable characters have few equals; and they are very hard to prosecute. But each year they take tens of millions of dollars from ordinary families by exploiting our very human penchant for believing in dreams of riches.

In the chapter, "The High-Pressure Pitch," we'll describe in detail how these "land butchers" work. Once you learn to recognize their lingo you'll have taken a long step toward preserving your hard-earned dollars. Where their "opportunities" are concerned, you have a much better chance of making a killing on a "tight" slot machine.

The chief appeal of unanchored raw land is its apparent bargain price. Drive through the open desert areas in the South, the Southwest and the West, and you'll see their signs:

PRIME LAND $500 AN ACRE!
LOW DOWN–EASY TERMS

We have seen these signs in Nevada, Arizona, New Mexico, Oklahoma, Texas, Arkansas and in eastern Oregon and Washington. When we go to the county seat to look up the records, invariably we find that the "land butcher" who has leveraged the deal and done nothing to the property but hack it up into two-and-one-half, five- and ten-acre parcels with a scraper— "ranch roads," he calls the raw scuff marks—nevertheless is charging up to twenty times what he paid for it. In fact, your down payment may cover his entire cost for that particular parcel. "Low down," indeed!

These are the peddlers who do absolutely nothing to enhance the value of the property, but whose crude subdivisions instantly raise the tax assessments because of the smaller parcels. What they want is your signature on a land sale contract—*not on a trust deed and note that gives you some legal protection too*— and as much cash down payment as they can squeeze out of you. After that they'll be content to collect your payments until you default, which you are likely to do when you wake up. Then they will take back the land and resell it to some other "yupper"* who comes long. Like the proverbial streetcar of yore, he knows another one will be along in a minute. We have seen raw parcels that have been sold five and six times because of repossession.

These operators are not to be confused with their more sophisticated brothers who actually make some effort to bring in power, develop water, surface a main access road and perhaps build a clubhouse and swimming pool or putting green, all of which are used as a sales office and can be written off by the developer.

To be absolutely fair, we have talked to people who made such purchases and seemed happy enough. They had hung on for years because the payments were modest and so were taxes. They admitted that as low as taxes were, over the term of the contract they probably paid the county as much as the land was really worth.

---

*Promoters' jargon for a sucker who stands there grinning and saying "Yup" to all the good things the con man is saying about his swindle.

While ethical realtors agreed that the land might be worth "somewhat more now," they were quick to add that no present market existed or likely would exist in the foreseeable future.

What will these buyers do? "It didn't cost all that much," they said. "We'll just hold it for the grandchildren."

Others said, "We never really believed all of that talk about cities and getting rich. We just wanted a piece of cheap land we could come and camp on once in a while. We figured a couple of thousand for two and a half acres was okay."

Still in the interests of fairness, we hasten to admit that the raw land picture is far from all bad. There is no practical way to list the areas where raw (undeveloped) land, marketed a decade or more ago, has actually fulfilled the promoter's promise of substantial profit to the purchaser.

Hundreds of such places do exist. We have visited them in almost every state of the union and in several Canadian provinces as well. In each case the increase in land value came about as the result of three influences:

1. A general up-valuing of land throughout the area.
2. "People pressure."
3. The extension of basic utilities to the area.

In *The Simple Truth about Western Land Investment* we used a number of graphic illustrations to show how "people pressure" exerts its value-boosting influence along the paths of least resistance. Those paths, of course, are the historic channels of communication discussed in Chapter Four—the channels along which our strip cities have developed. In more recent historical times those avenues of access were the railroads that opened up vast areas—usually land they themselves were given free by a grateful government as an inducement to build our national rail network.

In no place is that example more vivid than in California where the Southern Pacific Railroad's land company owns nearly 4 percent of the private holdings in the state—roughly 2 million acres ranging from dense forest land to the rich farmland of the San Joaquin Valley. The Southern Pacific holdings comprise an area roughly the size of the state of Maine. Any land policy decision made by such a giant owner can affect, adversely or otherwise, thousands of smaller landowners.

There is much political pressure now to break up these immense holdings so that a number of small agriculturists can have a chance to work the land under our free enterprise system. Idealistic though that theory may be, in practice when such holdings are fractured the prime pieces are usually picked up by the large corporate agriculturists and by corporate developers. Title and management simply passes from big to less big. Seldom does the small investor get a real chance at the best of it. If he is alert, however, he may pick up some valuable "crumbs from the land barons' table," for it is true that as much property as the railroads and mining companies and timber companies own, they do not own it all. But these days they do have a strong incentive to develop much of it. Their neighbors undoubtedly will profit too.

Raw land, held undeveloped in inventory for decades, has become a financial drain as tax assessors continue their search for new or expanded sources of public revenue. The railroads were among the first of the huge land holders to see the advantages of getting into the development business. Several railroads, among them the Burlington Northern (Big Sky, Montana) have taken strong positions in land development and their activities have helped greatly to increase land values in many areas. In the early monopolistic days, the railroads were not noted for their magnanimity. But in recent times, under the pressure of competition, some of them displayed what appears to be a genuine concern for the common good. The small investor who, through accident or foresight, found his holdings close by recreational and agricultural development generally has profited, even though his taxes may also have jumped several hundred percent in the ensuing years.

If, in this work, we seem to be qualifying the advantages of raw land investments, it is because it is somewhat more difficult for the small investor to find good open land now than it was even five years ago. There was raw palmetto land available for a few hundred dollars an acre just outside Orlando, Florida, little more than a decade ago.

In our earlier works we cited example after example of people whose "little place out in the country" suddenly became a veritable gold mine when the first suburban tentacles of the "megaloctopus" finally embraced them. This has happened from Los Angeles' San Fernando Valley to the extreme reaches of Long Island's Suffolk County and from Calumet, Michigan, to Key West, Florida, and all through the "heartland" as well. Moreover, we have recently visited areas where it has happened in France, Spain, Italy and in the Balearic Islands of Majorca, Minorca and Ibiza. To that one could add most of the lovely cities in Mexico and in South America—nor should we exclude Australia, New Zealand, and, of all places, the Fiji Islands.

The "People-Pressure Principle" (with apologies to author friend, Laurence J. Peter) is operative now in most of the urban centers of the world as our population expands and begins to move in ever increasing numbers outward along modern, but not always more efficient, transport channels. The point to remember is this: *Where people move outward, land prices move upward. Analyze the areas where that is most apt to happen and you've found a prime land investment area.*

There are a number of classic examples of "people pressure" forcing settlement and the upward evaluation of raw "jack-rabbit land." Witness the miracle of Phoenix, Arizona, and its galaxy of suburban satellites where solid rock, sand and cactus, mixed with water and power, has produced some of the most delightful and expensive real estate on earth. Visit Tucson and see the great circle of suburban sprawl that is now visible from the smart dining club atop its highest skyscraper. Add to that Albuquerque, New Mexico and the fabulous Dallas-Fort Worth corridor in Texas. Close by all of these places and many other lesser urban centers in the West and Southeast, what was once, "I-wouldn't-give-ya-a-nickel-fer-it" land is now selling by the square foot!

Of all the examples, none is more dramatic than that now being witnessed in Southern California's spectacular Antelope Valley where research led to a sizable personal investment in the Willow Springs area. A 2,500 square mile triangle of water-rich high desert, the valley seems to have been blessed with everything including gold, silver and platinum, and 360 days of flying weather every year. (More on that latter aspect when we talk about factors that send land prices soaring.)

Almost all of the Antelope Valley's 1,600,000 acres are usable. Bounded by the snow-covered 10,000-foot San Gabriel Mountains on the south and the equally dramatic pine-clad Tehachapi Range on the north and west, the valley is a huge fertile triangle that is still one of the richest agricultural areas in the West.

For fifty years, some of the state's finest alfalfa has been grown under irrigation in the valley. It is not unusual to get five cuttings during the nine-month growing season.

Herds of beef and dairy cattle graze in the western apex of the area that many call "The Emerald Triangle."

In the spring, tourists from all over the United States visit the breathtaking wildflower preserve below the historic settlement of Willow Springs to drive or wander on foot through several thousand acres of native California poppy and lupine.

By early summer, air passengers can look down on mile-long rows of self-propelled sprinklers irrigating thousands of acres of produce and alfalfa. The entire area is crisscrossed by a grid of modern paved roads. Cutting north and south through the heart of the richest part of the valley is the new Antelope Valley Freeway, one of the finest high-speed arteries in the United States. It links the Antelope Valley's growing cities with the Los Angeles megalopolis less than an hour's safe drive to the south.

Bisecting the valley is the east-west artery, Highway 138, scheduled to be a freeway also. This high-speed road connects Highway 395 at the eastern end of the Antelope Valley with the new Interstate 5 at Gorman on the west. Except for a few short segments in the Cascades and close to Tijuana, south of San Diego, this great international freeway is complete from Canada to Mexico.

On July 11, 1967, the Southern Pacific Railroad opened a seventy-eight-mile stretch of new track called the Palmdale-Colton Cutoff. It was the first major railroad construction in the West in forty years—a vital rail link that saves Antelope Valley shippers thousands of days of travel time each year.

With all of this going for it, surely it must be clear why we have chosen this particular area as an example. It is unique in that it contains all of the classic requisites for profitable expansion and the in-built potential for a solid increase in land values.

Summed up, they are as follows:

- Adjacency to one of the three largest metropolitan centers in the United States.

- Served by a network of ultramodern roads, rail transportation and air traffic facilities.

- Abundant level land.

- Abundant indigenous water, supplemented by a new aqueduct sufficient to supply its growth needs for decades. Readily available electricity and natural gas and a great proved mineral wealth.

- A very "livable climate."

- The logical "spillover area" for the Los Angeles megalopolis with almost unlimited space for broad-spectrum expansion ranging from agriculture to the most sophisticated of industries, aerospace (of which the valley is destined to become the national center).

- Adaptability to an ultramodern, conservation orientated, long-range master plan that will guarantee a compatible environment for all.

• The site of Edwards Air Force Base, one of the world's most advanced research and development facilities and the western headquarters of National Aeronautics and Space Administration (NASA).

At least four of those elements have been present in the Antelope Valley for many years. From time to time there would be minor increases in land values in and around its three principal communities—Palmdale, Lancaster and Mojave.

But it was not until shortly after World War II that the true potential of the great valley was generally understood. The wartime location of large segments of the aircraft industry provided the first impetus, just as it provided the final boost for the nearby San Fernando Valley.

The second stage was supplied by the aerospace program that began with the location of NASA at Edwards and the subsequent breaking of the sound barrier by the X-1 "rocket ship" and the resulting space hardware test programs that originated there.

Additional impetus was provided by the relocation of several large commercial industries in the valley. Thousands of aircraft and aerospace workers who had been commuting began shifting their residences to the exciting new, smog-free valley. Positive word of mouth worked its useful magic. More new industries came in and brought more new workers, and the vacancy factor in residential housing dropped to less than 3 percent.

Then came approval for the new freeway and funding for the unprecedented "Feather River Project"—the world's longest freshwater transport system. Close on this came rumors of a great new intercontinental airport at Palmdale that would incorporate parts of Air Force Plant 42 from whose two 10,000-foot runways the spectacular supersonic X-15 was successfully flown.

The "Westward Tilt," the name that San Diego *Evening Tribune* columnist and distinguished author, Neil Morgan, gave it in his 1961 best seller, began spilling its population from the overcrowded Los Angeles coastal shelf into the San Fernando "basin." Soon, more than a trickle began spilling another thirty miles northward into the Antelope Valley. The trickle became a stream as "people pressure"—really "back pressure" from the overcrowded basin—began to take effect.

A new strip city was beginning to move northward along Interstate 5 toward Bakersfield in the San Joaquin Valley. The western tip of the triangular Antelope Valley connected with the new six-lane, high-speed artery, and curious visitors began coming in from that direction.

On the south, at Saugus and Newhall, two once sleepy ranch communities, the congealed agony of old earth faults was concealed by giant earth-moving equipment preparing sites for a retirement city and a score of new subdivisions that were springing up along the new Antelope Valley Freeway. Inching ever closer, they are now the harbingers of what most observers feel will become the last and perhaps the largest megalopolis in the West.

It has taken a decade for this process to reach the point where it is now regarded as inevitable. As elsewhere, there have been a number of boom and bust cycles in the Antelope Valley during the past fifteen years. Most have resulted from the termination of military and aerospace contracts.

Real estate brokers and local booster organizations, behaving in an eminently human manner, envisioned "great things" for the valley, and their enthusiasm was infectious. (Some say they oversold the area but it seems clear now that history will vindicate them). Land prices soared, then nosedived again. But each time this happened a few more permanent inhabitants and a few more businesses put down roots. By 1966 Lancaster alone was served by more than 800 retail stores and financial institutions.

In August of 1968 when the Palmdale Intercontinental Airport was finally approved, everything hit the ceiling and a lot of it "stuck."

Perhaps nothing illustrates more vividly how these ups and downs work than the history of a single parcel of land that may be said to lie in the middle of things.

In 1955, this ten-acre parcel two miles west of downtown Lancaster (still unincorporated but the largest of the Antelope Valley communities) sold for $125 an acre. In 1960, when the freeway and water project both got the green light, the land resold for $350 an acre. In 1965, when "hard information" came that Lockheed was actually going to build its new commercial jet, the L-1011 Tri-Star, in a huge new facility at Palmdale, Lancaster's twin city just nine miles to the south, the property sold again, this time for $1,200 an acre.

There was another flurry of excitement when the first flow from the new aqueduct pumped northern California water over the Tehachapi Mountains from the San Joaquin Valley, and it then came snaking through the engineering marvel that is the Antelope Valley leg of the California State Water Project. Property on the south side of the valley jumped another hundred dollars an acre on the average.

Then, in February 1969, the Los Angeles City Council adopted a resolution in support of a land acquisition program that would put together the huge acreage needed for the Palmdale Intercontinental Airport. Buyers' tension grew as speculators and investors crowded into the valley looking for choice peripheral parcels.

In August of 1969 the California Department of Aeronautics approved the proposed airport site. The action was confirmed in Washington in June of 1970 by Secretary of Transportation John A. Volpe.

The ten-acre parcel we were monitoring went up like Professor Piccard's famous balloon. Three days later it sold for $5,000 an acre. In September of 1970 the 18,000 acre airport land acquisition began, and real estate values in the entire Antelope Valley and environs went "out through the roof." A general state of civic euphoria set in.

Then came the environmentalists. Seven Palmdale citizens who opposed the building of any airport in the area enlisted the sympathetic support of the Sierra Club. A law suit was filed charging illegal procedure, and the two billion dollar "P.I.A." project was stopped cold!

Stunned property owners walked around in a daze of disbelief. "How can seven soreheads stop a two billion dollar airport that we all need?" they asked. The answer, which they knew as well as anybody, was simple: In a democracy such as ours, one person can stop a project until the merits of his argument have been judged by due process.

There were angry threats and talk of vigilante action as land values continued to sag and speculators who had moved in filled with hope of a quick killing began to look for a way out. Taxes and assessments became liens on property already leveraged to the hilt. The number of defaults grew. Optimism faded and deep pessimism took its place. Men who should have known better predicted the "end" of the valley. But investors with cash who knew better, who understood human nature, moved in to buy. Some purposely aided and abetted the negative talk in order to encourage panicky speculators to sell at distress prices. Many did—and soon, land sales in general slowed to a walk as most buyers adopted a "wait and see" attitude.

Behind all of the legal maneuvering by the environmentalists was the contention that no satisfactory environmental impact report had been filed in compliance with the federal law before airport land acquisition began.

Concessions were made. Runways were relocated on plans to reduce the possibility of noise pollution. In July of 1971 the Department of Airports engaged the Arthur D. Little Company of San Francisco to conduct an environmental impact study. The pro-airport people expressed a willingness to abide by the results.

As this is being written a series of public hearings is taking place that will give the Arthur D. Little Company a broad input of public opinion that may well influence the final decision.

Most observers feel it will come in mid-1975. Meanwhile, land acquisition has begun again. As of January 15, 1973, more than 7,000 acres had been purchased.

Most thoughtful people now feel the Palmdale Intercontinental Airport will be built because it must be. "People pressure"—or in this case, "passenger pressure"—has made it mandatory that Los Angeles have another major airport. Just as New York City outgrew LaGuardia Airport and was forced to build Idlewild (now John F. Kennedy) Airport, so has Los Angeles outgrown LAX.

Those who are angered by the action of the Sierra Club and "The Palmdale Seven" claim their obstructions were unjustified, that all of the necessary environmental considerations had been incorporated in the original plan. True, most of them were. Even as it originally stood, the airport was a marvel of planning. But a lot of valid peripheral problems remained to be solved, not the least of which was some form of rapid transit to get passengers to and from the Antelope Valley into the San Fernando Valley and into Los Angeles' downtown heart.

The new Antelope Valley Freeway right-of-way offers one logical route. Another, needing some new engineering, is the present right-of-way of the Southern Pacific Railroad that not only serves the heavily populated San Fernando Valley but also terminates at Union Station in downtown Los Angeles.

The blues are still being sung by small investors and professional speculators who went in over their heads only to see their "improbable dreams" go a-glimmering. But more far-sighted "valleyites" took a calmer view.

"Sure, we wish the whole legal mess hadn't happened," one broker said. "But it could be that we moved too fast. After all, we've been dreaming this dream for a long time. It's only natural to want things to go. Nothing gets built by saying you *can't* do it. We're hurting right now. But when this thing gets cleared up in the courts, this valley is really going to take off—with nothing but green lights out ahead." Then he added, a bit contritely. "We've damned the hell out of the conservationists, but when things do start to go, it will be under a master plan that will make this one of the modern and livable areas in the country. That's for sure. And one of the best investment places too," he added, "because you can't separate value from good planning. That's something we all have to learn."

As this is being written (February 1973), the Los Angeles Department of Airports has released the results of a careful study of job impact that will be created by the new Palmdale Intercontinental Airport. The figures, while conservative, are impressive:

> More than 35,000 new jobs at the airport itself;
> More than 10,000 new jobs in office buildings nearby;
> More than 87,500 related retail and restaurant jobs;
> More than 6,000 construction jobs;
> More than 300,000 increase in area population ("people pressure");
> More than $350 million increase in payrolls during construction.

This is the stuff that value is made of! This sort of value-boosting development is relative to the area. Wherever a *valid need* is recognized and a demand for services is being met, values must rise. That is as true of the new Grand Teton ski resorts as it is of a huge new intercontinental airport needed to serve one of the three largest megalopolises in the country. It becomes a matter of degree, but in either instance the new economic dynamics provide interesting investment opportunities for the "average family" that will pick its spot and follow up.

In north-central Washington State another example of a classic investment opportunity is shaping up in the rich but hitherto remote Methow (Met'-how) Valley. Lying 120 airline miles northeast of Seattle across the Cascade Range and about the same distance northwest of Spokane across the Okanogan

Range, the fifty-mile-long serpentine valley is one of the most beautiful and unspoiled areas in the United States.

For a half century the spectacular mountain valley has been known as a sportsman's paradise. Two rivers, the Twisp and the Chewack, and a dozen year-around creeks, flow into the Methow River which, in turn, flows southward to join the Columbia at the apple-packing center of Pateros.

Apples, potatoes and feed crops thrive in the Methow's soil. Lumbering has long been a major industry centered at the picturesque little town of Twisp, an Indian name meaning "Yellow Jacket." From Twisp, south to the Columbia River, some of the nation's finest apple orchards grow along the curving margins of the Methow River.

Each summer, fishermen in campers and motor homes converge on the valley to take prize rainbow trout from its streams and from the mountain lakes nestled in the Alpine fastness of the surrounding Cascades and the Okanogans.

In the autumn the hunters arrive to shoot pheasant and chukar and to stalk the deer that abound in the region in such numbers that farmers and orchardists are frequently issued special licenses to keep the population down.

Then, in 1958, largely through the prolonged efforts of local residents who wanted to see the area progress, a project was initiated that now promises great changes for the valley.

For three decades the ranchers and farmers in the Methow had been trying to secure government financing for a direct road westward across the Cascade Range to the Pacific Slope and the deep-water port of Anacortes. Without such access they were forced to ship much of their beef, sheep, lumber and produce over two hundred miles of tortuous road to Seattle.

In 1962 the project was finally funded and construction began. Then years later, in September of 1972, the new North Cascades Highway was dedicated and the first trickle of campers began to flow over the mountain passes on the spectacular new artery that followed Early Winters Creek down into the Methow.

The United States Forest Service, anticipating a rapidly increasing flow of vacationers, estimated $900,000 would be needed for new campgrounds and a visitors' center at Early Winters, the point where the new highway enters the valley.

In anticipation of increased tourist traffic, a group of local men built *Sun Mountain Lodge,* a modern, beautifully conceived rustic resort and convention center on a timbered highland overlooking the valley, two of its rivers and several nearby lakes. An expansion program is planned that will include condominium second-home recreational dwellings.

Another group, alert to the possibilities for development that follow the construction of such a highway, filed tract maps for second-home recreational developments. A thirty-acre site was bought for a shopping center. Several new ski resorts are in the planning stage to supplement the newly developed Loup Loup Recreational Area in the Okanogans, the valley's eastern "wall." At least three new motels are in various stages of development to meet an acute shortage of accommodations.

A group of Seattle investors has purchased a three-mile-long parcel of land fronting on the Methow River. Their plan also includes second-home recreational residences. Other investors, sensing the need for restaurants, stores, service stations and other commercial installations, are scouting the valley for choice locations.

It is not surprising that land prices have risen. In those areas zoned for commercial services, preferred locations have changed from a *per acre* price to a *front foot* price. Much of it is going at $50 a front foot—up 50 percent in the past year.

River frontage has risen from $500 an acre to $1,500, depending upon timber, terrain and location. Good timbered land back from the rivers has risen from $150 an acre to the $750 range. Well-timbered slopes with fine views of the valley and streams are selling in the $1,000 an acre range—with location again a factor.

Determined that the in-migration of new residents and the influx of tourists will not bring about unbridled development, the local residents who masterminded the highway are now working with county authorities to develop a master plan that will preserve the valley's prime agricultural land and insure orderly development of resorts and residences in appropriate areas.

One of the Methow's primary needs, despite new Forest Service camps and new National Park facilities (the new highway is the only access to the park), is a number of well-conceived, privately owned recreational vehicle parks.

Some indication of the need for privately developed recreational vehicle facilities can be gained from the U.S. Forest Service and National Park Service traffic estimates over the new highway. The Forest Service studies, made in 1968, four years before the highway was opened, were conservative indeed. They showed an average daily traffic flow of 1,650 vehicles per day. Each vehicle was estimated to carry 2.65 passengers. Summer traffic was estimated at 5,600 vehicles daily, each carrying 3.5 persons.

In the sixty-day period following the actual opening of the North Cascades Highway on September 1, 1972, more than *one-quarter of a million persons* made the spectacular seventy-four mile, one hour and twenty minute drive from Diablo Dam on the Pacific Slope of the mountains to Twisp, the commercial and tourist center of the valley. National Park Service projections, corrected for 1973, anticipate *three-quarters of a million visitors.* On the basis of these projections, historically conservative, it seems safe to predict that the Methow Valley will soon be experiencing a new kind of "People Pressure" generated by a horde of mobile Americans. They will be dedicated to enjoying their expanded leisure time in the unpolluted, indescribably beautiful North Cascade Primitive Area, in the North Cascades National Park, in the Okanogan National Forest and in the Methow Valley which lies at the heart of it all. Those of us who love the valley can only hope that the progressive residents who brought about this change will prove equal to the challenge of orderly development and will resist the "greenback" blandishments of the speculators who always appear to exploit and usually to despoil these newly opened areas of great natural beauty.

No matter what one's political persuasion, nearly everybody agrees that the economic indicators for the next few years are hopeful. Regardless of who eventually deserves to take the bow, the country is "turning around." The tragedy of Vietnam may have ended with the "Cease Fire" agreement. In any case, a good part of what will happen to this country during the remainder of the 1970s will depend upon our attitude. Unmistakably, there are signs that it is taking a positive turn. America seems ready to tackle some of its own urgent problems with renewed will. If that is true, the result will be a greatly strengthened economy. Solid investment opportunities will result, and foremost among them will be investment opportunities in land.

Southern California's Antelope Valley and the Dallas-Fort Worth corridor are by no means the only "hot" areas. Neither is Washington State's Methow Valley. A book that attempted to list even the most obvious of them would soon get out of hand. We have no doubt that readers of these pages will recognize many areas close to home where promising indicators exist. These indicators are as obvious as Marriott's new "Great America" theme park near Columbia, Maryland; or the "Worlds of Fun" international theme park to be developed near Kansas City by Lamar Hunt and his associates; or the proposed new theme park near Richmond, Virginia, being planned for a 1975 opening by the Taft Broadcasting Company and Top Value Enterprises, a subsidiary of Kroger. One has only to recall Disneyland and Disney World to sense the possibilities for those who are alert to the first rumors of such projects, who trouble to check them out and who act if they seem to have substance.

Land for great projects such as Disney World often takes years to put together. Usually it is done secretly through "front organizations" acting as cover-up agents. The reason for this subterfuge is obvious. (Disney learned it the hard way at Anaheim, California!) The mere rumor that such a major attraction or other economic asset is to be built is sufficient to send land prices skyrocketing.

Disney World's "front" brokers, sworn to CIA-like secrecy, took several years to put together the Orlando acreage needed for the attraction itself and the 27,000 acres needed for the various Disney-owned or influenced installations peripheral to it! By the time the public announcement was made, the land had all been acquired. However, the small investor need not despair. The "ground effect" of such high-impact development can be felt for miles around. If he acts promptly and does his homework well, there is still time for a profitable investment reasonably nearby.

John and Jane Doe are probably not going to become Mr. and Mrs. Super-Dough unless they were fortunate enough to own a substantial acreage at "ground zero" and unless they were shrewd enough to suspect something was up and not jump at the first blind offer that came along. That takes the "gut conviction" that comes from research. But John and Jane may very well become Mr. and Mrs. J. Dough, Esquire, if they move and acquire a few acres or lots adjacent to the developing area and are willing to wait.

In Florida, those who are still kicking themselves for not having bought south of Orlando, in Orange and Osceola Counties, may still find bargains to the north and east in Seminole County where "back pressure" from Disney World and other developments is sparking a secondary strip city that could reach all the way to Daytona and the Atlantic Coast.

The entire Orlando "hub," in transition from prime agricultural and cattle-raising enterprises to recreational and service orientated activities, is exerting a far-reaching influence. Retirees who used to comprise the majority of the new population are now a minority, outnumbered by a vast migration of new, younger residents.

During 1971 and 1972, 60,000 new residents came into the area (40,000 more are projected for 1973). In 1972 this in-migration resulted in 19,000 new jobs in the Orlando area--the highest increase in the nation.

Multiple real estate listings for 1972 showed an average value increase of $5,000 per home. In that single twelve-month period, the average sales price of a private residence increased from $23,000 to $28,000. It has not topped out yet.

We were told by an unimpeachable source of one grove owner fifteen miles south of Orlando who paid $200 an acre for his land in 1946. In 1971, just twenty-five years later, he sold it to a conglomerate for $200,000 an acre. That's right--$200,000 an acre. He was at "ground zero"!

Not all of the local old-timers are happy about the change taking place in the Orlando area. But as one civic organization officer said, "At least they're weeping all the way to the bank. Some of the rest of us don't like it all that much either. But we'd much rather have it this way than to have the area go stagnant. And if we really want to leave, we can get out with enough money to comfort us in our old age elsewhere."

The growth in the Orlando area is not all tied to recreation and service. There has been an influx of industry too. Stromberg-Carlson, Ralston-Purina, Chrysler Corporation, General Electric and Brunswick are among the dozens of corporations that have located in the area. The solid industrial tax base they represent lends substance to the boom.

In truth, spectacular growth may be a mixed blessing. There is a historic lag between the time a boom is recognized and the time it takes to create an organization strong enough to contain it. In Orlando, the East Central Florida Regional Planning Council was formed and is now drafting a master plan designed to stop helter-skelter growth that results from uncoordinated planning in surrounding communities. It is no easy task! Honest differences of opinion and other motives not so honest all must be handled. The problem is universal, as unwary New England is finding out.

To the dismay of many Vermonters, for instance, the second-home recreational residence boom is creating a "people-pressure" situation in Burlington and environs. Alarmed at what has happened elsewhere, the state has now passed one of the country's toughest master plans. While it has not entirely stopped the exploitation of some of its most beautiful recreational regions, the plan guarantees controlled development, sensible density and responsible preservation of those special esthetic qualities that make Vermont one of the most beautiful of states. This has been accomplished without adversely affecting the profit potential for those investors and developers who are wise enough to understand that *sensible planning* is not restrictive. On the contrary, it virtually guarantees increased real estate values.

In Texas the construction of the world's largest and most modern airport in the Dallas-Fort Worth corridor has resulted in a positive financial fallout in such small nearby communities as Lewisville, Coppell, Irving and Grapevine. In fact, the town of Irving got a double dose of "horseshoe luck" when the Dallas Cowboys chose it as the site of their new 65,000 seat stadium. Draw a circle with a fifty-mile radius around the new airport and you will still be at or near "ground zero," so far as the explosive impact on future development is concerned.

Ten years from now, with the development of a new rapid-transit concept, it is likely that the positive impact will be felt for one hundred miles around. In Texas a hundred miles is "just down the road a piece—and you-all drop in and see us this evenin' after work."*

In the search for raw speculative or investment land that may, some years in the future, turn into a strip city or a "hot" area, one must bear in mind that our new preoccupation with ecological matters and conservation adds a new element to the quest. It may not be enough now to hear a rumor, check it out

---

*One of the great pleasures of researching by car in Texas was their "Drive Friendly" campaign. How we wished it would spread west to California!

and hasten to be the first to buy in for a ride up. The rumor may be true. All of the indicators may check out. The most conservative heads in the area may urge you to take an early position. And still you can run into unforeseen problems that can alter the entire worth of a deal.

Several striking examples come to mind in Florida and in California. Near Miami a huge new international airport was stopped cold by environmentalists who predicted that the development would mean the destruction of hundreds of thousands of acres of the Everglades. A lot of golden dreams turned to nightmares, for there are few *money magnets* that equal a major airport with its need for nearby hotels, restaurants, shops, offices, parking, car rental concerns and a hundred other subordinate services.

In California the Walt Disney organization finds itself caught in a bitter legal battle with environmentalists who are opposing plans to build an all-year resort at Mineral King in Southern California's High Sierra.

A dozen ski resorts in as many Western states have been frozen in blueprints pending further environmental impact studies. The regional head of a militant conservationist group stated flatly that the organization intended to use every available dollar to "study these developments to death."

Suits filed by environmentalists are clogging our courts. In September 1972, Chief Justice Warren F. Burger warned that the "explosive increase" in cases is apt to swamp the courts. No small part of this increase stems directly from these environmental disputes.

A news story in the January 30 issue of the *Los Angeles Times* reported that $200 million in claims have been filed against the state of California, the state of Nevada and the bi-state Tahoe Regional Planning Agency by developers and investors who contend that the new regional master plan has down-valued their property. Nevada estimates that it will have to find $100,000 just to pay its end of the court costs.

The warning is clear and so are the implications for the small investor or speculator who hopes to secure his future by holding to the tail of the "big boys' kite." Just being big does not guarantee special privilege or immunity in this conservation struggle. We mortals, being what we are, will probably always be able to point to instances where some big operator has managed to get "wired in" at city hall or at the state capital. But unless the small "me too" speculator is certain of the man he is following, he may find too late that his bellwether is, in fact, a Judas goat leading him to slaughter.

In general, undeveloped land still carries a higher profit potential than almost any other sort of real estate available to the small investor. But it also carries a disproportionate element of risk for those who do not do their investigating before they buy. That is why we feel constrained to observe that it may be wiser, therefore, if the average family makes its investment in an area where the land use planning has been completed, after making certain that the restrictions are compatible with the family investment objectives.

In time, "people pressure" will bring about modifications in present land use patterns covering land in remote open country, particularly if the area seems likely to be in the path of new progress. That may result in up-zoning. Up-zoning can herald an increase in property values. Inevitably, an increase in value means an increase in taxes, and that is worth remembering.

Unless part of the fun of the investment is the researching, scouting and comparing that must precede a purchase, a family will most likely be safer and happier going along with a reputable large developer who has already fought and won the environmental battle for his project. Cynics say, "A raw land investment is a speculation on which you guessed right." There is a certain ironic humor in that observation. But we'd rather say, "A prudent investor is one who leaves nothing to guesswork." The whole purpose of this book is to show a prospective buyer how to take the guesswork out of land investment.

46. *Five miles northwest of Kingman, Arizona, an area of remarkable growth, is this small "development." Ten years earlier, when we first visited the area led there by billboards proclaiming an exciting new community, the main street had just been scraped into being . . . a process that must be repeated after each heavy storm. Strangely enough, the residents in their sprinkling of mobile homes seem content with their investment. Davis Dam and Lake Mohave on the Colorado River are 30 miles to the west over State Highway 68. This would be a fair example of a recreational investment in which a family should reckon a good part of the "profit" in pleasure derived.*

47. Ten minutes from the "superdevelopment" at Sunriver, is this "Ma and Pa" subdivision. The Deschutes River is off through the trees to the left. The road is undedicated. Local residents said it evolved from fisherman's tracks. No utilities are near any of the "lots" we saw. The land is cheap and the area is beautiful; but a purchaser must be realistic about what he or she expects of this sort of investment. It is better suited for Recreational Vehicle use than second-home development. Such use would keep taxes down also.

48. September, 1972. First traffic across the spectacular North Cascades Highway that joins the Pacific Coast communities with the rich, beautiful Methow Valley. Penetrating thousands of square miles of "mountain-man country," the new highway is a boon to sportsmen's families and farmers and lumbermen alike. [Photograph courtesy of Wenatchee Daily World.]

49. Washington State's North Cascades Highway during final grading in Fall of 1971. [Photograph courtesy of Wenatchee Daily World.]

NOTICE OF SALE
PRIVATE PARTIES-INVESTORS
RANCH LIQUIDATION
(BY OWNER)
Priced at wholesale . . .Starting at
$85 PER ACRE

Entire ranch consisting of over 20,000 acres in Northern Arizona must be sold immediately! This working cattle ranch is located near Hwy. 66 (I-40) and is priced at wholesale in parcels of 160 acres or larger. Low down payment with up to 10 years on balance. Ideal for resale, investment and/or recreation. Hurry for choice selections.

50. Evidence of the problems some large ranchers find themselves in as a result of rising taxes, increasing labor costs, escalating shipping charges and inflation.

We do not know that any or all of these factors prompted this owner to sell. But many large ranchers, unable to operate economically in today's financial climate, are selling to individuals and to developers, taking their capital gains and reinvesting in less hazardous pursuits. Some ranchers turned developers!

In addition to the subscriptions to newspapers in the areas that interest you, one of the most effective sources of good information we have found is a bimonthly publication called *The Recreation Land and Leisure Housing Report,* published by the Housing Data Bureau, Post Office Box 97, Los Altos, California, 94022.

The annual subscription is $55.00 for twenty-four copies, roughly $2.30 an issue. This proves to be very cheap insurance since the report covers the entire United States and some foreign countries as well. Despite the title, the report is not limited to recreation land and leisure housing, but also carries general news of legislation at state and federal levels that is extremely useful to a prospective land investor. It is a professional publication. Most developers subscribe to it. But we know of no more useful publication for the small investor who wishes to keep up with all of the events that may affect his decision to buy. An inquiry will bring you a sample copy at no cost and a subscription blank to use if you wish.

"A little bit of knowledge" has always been "a dangerous thing." Where investing the family "nest egg" is concerned, it can be fatal. There is such a thing as *too little* good information; but there is no such thing as *too much* good information. If you do not balk at the idea of studying some, you'll soon find out that the research will lead you into some exciting new adventures. In the process you'll also learn some history, past and present, and quite probably will learn to appreciate this remarkable country of ours even more. And especially right now, we all need to appreciate Her!

17.
The "Reets" or
Real Estate Investment Trusts

If you would like to own some valuable real estate but feel that you cannot devote the time to the basic research that must be done to make a sound investment; and if you feel that you do not have sufficient money to make an "important" investment, then the new REIT—Real Estate Investment Trust—could be an interesting possibility to examine.

There are two types of "Reets," as they are known in the investment world. There is the *equity* type in which the shareholder actually owns a pro rata share of some real property—an office building, a shopping mall, an apartment building, a condominium second-home development and the like. And there is the *mortgage* type in which the shareholder becomes a pro rata "lender" of development money in much the same manner a bank or a savings and loan institution lends out mortgage money.

Although this is purely a matter of personal preference, we prefer the equity type "Reet" and in the following paragraphs will attempt to explain simply how a relatively complicated form of real estate investment works.

In order to understand the advantages a Real Estate Investment Trust offers the small investor over some of the other options open to him, we will use a couple of examples. A stockholder in a corporation is called a shareholder. A person who purchases a unit in a REIT is a shareholder of beneficial interest. As such, the investor purchases one or more shares in the trust.

Let us assume that an investor buys a share in one of the automobile manufacturing corporations. The share is purchased for two reasons; in the hope that it will increase in value and that it will produce some income through payment of dividends.

Using an average performance history, let us say that Corporation X shows gross earnings of 14 percent on its annual sales. Half of that, or 7 percent, is immediately subject to a federal corporation tax. That leaves a 7 percent net profit.

On the average, 3 percent of that money will be reinvested in the company and will, hopefully, increase the company's asset value by a like amount.

That leaves 4 percent to be distributed to shareholders as a dividend. But the individual shareholder's personal income tax rate will be applied to that 4 percent because it is regarded as income.

Now, if we assume that the 3 percent reinvested by the company in its capital assets increases the value of the individual shareholder's stock by 3 percent, that person will ultimately be able to take a capital gain on the amount.

If the shareholder is in a 50 percent tax bracket, he keeps 2 percent.

If he is in a 25 percent bracket, he keeps 3 percent.

If we ignore the capital gains tax for a moment, it is fair to say that the most the shareholder can make on the investment is 6 percent—or about the same return to be had in a Certificate of Deposit in a conventional bank or in a savings and loan institution.

The problem is, of course, that inflation is eroding the actual value of that 6 percent. Moreover, as our economy has been in recent years, there is no guarantee that Corporation X is going to earn enough after taxes to pay out a dividend equal to 4 percent of its earnings. This could affect the *book value* or *actual worth* of the share.

During the last twenty years a number of small investors have turned to the mutual funds as a way of diversifying so that all of their eggs are not in one corporate basket. Those who have held and continued to buy—who have "plowed back capital gains"—have done very well, by and large. But even so, because of the uncertain state of the national and world economies, many a mutual fund shareholder has decided to sell. For many months some large mutual funds have been "buying back" more shares than they have been selling, creating a "negative cash flow" that seriously affects the value of shares by limiting the fund's ability to reinvest.

So while the mutual fund has been a relatively safe and stable vehicle that allows the small investor to "spread his bets," few if any of them offer real tax shelter and the income, both regular and capital gains, is payable either by the fund management, or the shareholder—or both.

Income derived from conventional savings accounts will vary with the institution and the part of the country. But, generally speaking, a passbook savings account will draw from 4.75 percent to 5 percent. Time Deposits or Certificates of Deposit which require both a minimum deposit—sometimes as small as $500—and a minimum length of time before withdrawal, pay from 5.5 percent to 6 percent and the interest is regarded as regular income and is taxed as such. And these income dollars, too, are eroded by the annual inflation rate.

It was the in-built disadvantages in these more conventional forms of investment that set some bright young financial men to thinking about ways that a small investor might enjoy the same diversity and profit potential that the "big boys" enjoy in real estate investment. In the late 1950s their creative thinking led to the formulation of the real estate investment trust.

In 1960 the Congress, impressed with the possibility the plan offered for stimulating the economy with large infusions of private capital from small investors, passed The Real Estate Investment Trust Act, "Rita" as it is affectionately known by its admirers. Thus, a new avenue of possible income and profit for the small investor was officially "blessed."

Robert G. Lucas, senior partner of Lucas & Meyer, one of the pioneer consultants and counselors in this new type of real estate investment, calls the REIT the "ideal" investment for the "little man" and has expressed his reason for feeling so in an amusing acrostic.

Income
Depreciation
Equity buildup
Appreciation ·
Liquidity

Lucas, who acts as a consultant and counselor for the trustees of the REIT and the selling organizations such as the nationwide International Securities Corporation, makes this point:

As long as the government allows straight-line depreciation, the REIT offers to the small investor all of the economic and tax advantages of a major, broadly diversified investment in prime income-producing properties that formerly was available only to the very wealthy.

As things now stand, so far as the *equity trust* is concerned that would appear to be an accurate statement. In our own research into "Reets," we found five advantages:

1. An opportunity to conserve both capital and purchasing power.
2. A high potential rate of return.
3. A practical and legal tax shelter.
4. A remarkable potential for appreciation commensurate with management's effectiveness.
5. A workable hedge against inflation.

The objective of the equity real estate investment trust is to construct a vehicle for the average investor that can accomplish the following:

Earn up to 14 percent;
Legally shelter income from current taxes;
Pay its income directly to its shareholders;
Retain 6 percent of invested capital for *reinvestment;*
Pay up to 8 percent to shareholders in dividends;
Provide a sound depreciation schedule;
Provide proven management and administration.

Of the half dozen "Reets" examined, most had delivered on all counts. There is one point that the small investor should be clear about: No form of investment can absolutely guarantee a profit—not even a chain mortician whose supply of "product" has been underwritten "On High"!

Some "Reets" have been known to advertise themselves as "tax-free" vehicles. No way! The best a REIT can do is to convert ordinary income into future capital gains while increasing the investors' equity in the trust. In the end, the "little boys" like the "big boys" must pay. But how much sweeter it is to pay at the capital gains rate!

Now let's look at the basic elements of a good equity trust: We'd say the quality of management is paramount. All mortals are fallible. But those women and men in management whose track records prove that they have made fewer serious errors in judgment than most are the ones most apt to administer a successful operation.

Next, we would look for management that places the emphasis on diversification in acquiring real estate properties for the trust. Specialization narrows the opportunity and widens the chance for making mistakes. (In the sense that they espouse the diversified investment principle, the mutual funds are right.)

Our ideal REIT would have top management that tries to acquire only proven income producers that meet their minimum investment requirements. Some examples? A well-located shopping complex holding long-term leases with an important supermarket chain or a J. C. Penney or Sears; a Montgomery Ward or comparable quality tenants; a Sheraton Hotel or Motel; or, again, a comparable corporation whose standing guarantees payment of rental or lease or "lease back" income: these are only a few examples of quality tenants.

A REIT may own a shopping mall, an office building, a mobile home park, a condominium complex in a proven residential or recreational area, and it may own apartment houses in carefully chosen localities where rental factors indicate a good and continuing market.

To explain how the "machinery" of a REIT works to provide these tax and cash advantages to its shareholders, we'll call in our old friend "John Doe." (He aspires to change his name to John Dough!)

John Doe has decided to invest $1,000 in the Opportunity Knocks Real Estate Investment Trust, hereafter known as "The OK Trust." The following things happen:

> The management receives John Doe's check and banks it.
>
> Management immediately borrows $3,000 more.
>
> It will now buy $4,000 worth of income-producing properties.
>
> Management will begin to collect rent from the properties from which it must meet certain expenses: As any home owner or landlord know, real properties require maintenance. Then, management must be paid a salary or management fee. Taxes must be paid, and also office overhead expenses.
>
> Interest must be paid on the borrowed $3,000, and the note must be reduced by payments on principal.
>
> In a soundly conceived, well-managed REIT, after current expenses and taxes have been met, management should show a 2 percent cash surplus.

This 2 percent will translate to $80 (2 percent on $4,000).

John Doe will receive a check for $80 or an *8 percent* return on his $1,000 of invested capital. The REIT, can pay out that 8 percent in tax-sheltered cash because the law provides that to the extent depreciation is available on the holdings, the cash payment to the shareholder is sheltered from *current* taxation.

It is important to pay attention to the word *current.* If John Doe decides to sell his shares in the open market (they are traded on most exchanges), he will pay capital gains on the full amount he receives. But his $1,000 may now be worth $4,000.

If we use 8 percent as an arbitrary example (based on the actual performance of several good REITs) we see that in twelve and a half years our shareholder has been paid back his $1,000, and he still owns his full shares in the REIT (which quite likely are now worth considerably more).

How do the shares become worth more? Usually in two ways:

First, the REIT is reducing the $3,000 mortgage by 2 percent annually. That equals 6 percent on John Doe's invested $1,000. And that is regarded as an increase in equity—an increase in his share of the trust.

This 6 percent equity increase, plus the 8 percent he received by check, *amounts to a total of 14 percent return on his money, all of which is sheltered from current taxation.*

If you like figures and are following this, you'll see immediately that none of the foregoing assumes *one red cent of increase* in the overall value of the trust's properties. That is being ultraconservative. But we could find no dependable "average figure" to measure appreciation in value. Historically, however, prime income-producing property such as a well-managed REIT would own has always appreciated.

It is safe to say that a good property will increase in value at least as fast as the rate of inflation because of the increased cost of replacement.

So John Doe's 14 percent return, already sheltered against current taxes, is further hedged against inflation because the return is being paid on an asset base that is increasing at least as fast as the rate of inflation.

So now, when you pass the forbidding facade of the VIP Club and see those distinguished, graying millionaires savoring cigars and brandy and talking smugly about how they got rich, you, John Dough, will be "in the know," for the REIT is Everyman's key to the hallowed halls of high finance.

As with any other sort of investment, some real estate investment trusts are better than others, and all should be looked into carefully before committing the $10 a share that most of them regard as the minimum unit.

First of all, it is best to buy into a REIT at its *equity asset value*. That means buy into a *new* one, not an old one that is selling at a premium. In a new REIT the market value and the book value are the same.

Second, look for a "REET" that has a programmed method of property acquisition that is going to span a long period of time. This is important because ideally you want the management to acquire properties at about the same rate as its incoming cash flow from the sale of shares. In this way, management will not have a sudden embarrassment of riches that it will have to invest hastily to produce a return.

Third, make certain the management policy is one of *sound diversification* so that any risk will be spread over a number of good properties.

Fourth, make certain that management does not take more than *15 percent maximum* for operating expense. That figure, by the way, is the maximum allowed by law. Most good REITs operate for substantially less.

If this is the first time you've heard of a REIT, a real estate investment trust, or if it's the first time you've had one explained, then you have probably just discovered what an increasing number of small investors are discovering: that you can play in the big game for small chips and, proportionately, enjoy the same opportunities to shelter current dollars and increase your capital as those enjoyed by the most distinguished names on Wall Street.

But remember—with "Reets," as with any investment—investigate before you invest! And while you're doing that, satisfy yourself as to the liquidity (salability) of your shares on the open market in case an emergency arises and you need cash. Remember that fluctuation is the normal state of any sort of security or commodity market. The "Reet" shares do not seem as likely to move up or down as those common stocks that are constantly pressured by transient economic factors and by buyers' whims and hunches. But they can move down as well as up.

18.
The Real Estate Syndicate

If you are a doctor, a lawyer or a successful actor you probably know a lot about real estate syndicates. They have been growing in popularity ever since the 1950s, and their popularity bears a direct relationship to the Internal Revenue Service's continuing efforts to close the few tax loopholes still available to the individual "wage earner."

In its simplest form the real estate syndicate is a sort of mutual fund of ready cash which a number of "limited partners" (individuals who participate in the syndicate) supply to the "general partner," the promoter who dreamed up the syndicate and who makes its real estate purchases and sales and provides management.

The basic idea behind the syndicate is to create deductions and a tax shelter—and possibly a capital gains—for the limited partners who are in individual income tax brackets that "hurt."

For instance, a married couple with a $100,000 annual income will probably pay somewhere in the neighborhood of $45,000 in federal income taxes. If they are members of a successful syndicate and their share of interest paid on the syndicate's mortgaged indebtedness is $20,000, they can deduct that amount. Their tax can drop as much as $15,000, which is a substantial savings.

If they are fortunate enough to be in a well-managed syndicate and the properties are later sold for a profit, their share of the capital gains represents an offset against straight income and, hence, represents an indirect tax savings.

Like the real estate investment trust, the syndicate operates on borrowed money. But unlike the 25 percent base equity maintained by the best "Reets," the real estate syndicate may be leveraged by as much as 90 percent on some deals.

More than that, whereas the "Reet" management is prohibited by law from taking more than 15 percent fee for operations, the syndicate general partner, whose operations are usually under the jurisdiction of a state corporation commissioner, may take 50 percent and more for his various services. The regulations vary from state to state, and the part that the Securities and Exchange Commission plays in overall regulation of real estate syndicates is far from clear.

On occasion a disproportionate amount of money has gone directly into the pockets of the syndicate operators. That is not to say that the general partners have pocketed the money for doing nothing. It is simply that some of them have charged exorbitant fees for their services. This can be done in a number of ways:

> The promoter or general partner may charge the limited partners a broker's fee for locating the property.
> He may charge another fee for running the syndicate.
> And another fee for arranging the mortgage on the buildings.
> And still another fee for managing the properties.

The SEC is said to have received one syndication plan that called for the promoters to keep over sixty-five cents of every dollar collected from the limited partners. As one disillusioned doctor in the syndicate said, "And I couldn't even take the sonuvabitch off as a dependent!"

While a number of syndicates have operated very successfully for years and have accomplished their objectives for the limited partners, it is equally true that others have proved to be spectacular failures.

The loan officer of one Southern California bank got so mesmerized by the glowing promises of a real estate promoter that he approved between six and eight million dollars in mortgage loans in a three-year period.

When the syndicate, deeply leveraged in apartment houses, fell on troubled times as a result of high vacancy factors, the bank officer resigned and the shocked directors who had relied on his judgment immediately threatened legal action against the limited partners to recover the bank's money. This occurred despite the fact that the limited partners were promised that they had little or no liability.

Settlements undoubtedly will be made. In the end the apartment rental situation may turn around, and the properties may be sold for enough to satisfy the lender. In the meantime, the limited partners are going through some very nervous times. One psychiatrist who was a limited partner said ruefully, "I'm spending a lot of time on my own couch lately. Over and over, I'm asking myself, 'Why, Mervin—why?' "

It is not our intention here to discredit the real estate syndicate. We repeat, there are many solid ones that are performing admirably. We know of one that controls $3 million worth of real estate with a 20 percent equity. The mortgages were taken out at a time when the prime rate was 6 percent, and the syndicate got "preferred investor" treatment by the bank.

The general partner is a tax lawyer who holds a real estate broker's license. He is also a qualified appraiser. He pays competent managers in the apartment and medical buildings the syndicate owns, and his office staff consists of "two sharp girls."

The six limited partners, lawyers and doctors, could not be more delighted. In fact they have urged their general partner to expand the syndicate. Being a prudent man who knows his own capacity for careful work, he has refused.

That syndicate will operate efficiently for as many years as the general partner is able and willing to assume his responsibilities. The fee for his expert services is 20 percent.

Compared to the REIT the real estate syndicate is a relatively simple investment vehicle, and this factor can be one of its assets. Against that is the usual lack of diversity. As we have seen, there is a close inverse relationship between diversity and risk.

Again, we cannot emphasize too strongly the role of management. A syndicate may be said to be as good as the judgment of its general partner. The limited partners seldom take an active interest in the management of their syndicate. Since they are usually "high-bracket" professional people or executives, their main interest lies in effecting a tax savings. As a professional, they accord their general partner the same confidence they demand of their own patients and clients.

The real estate syndicate we have been referring to thus far is one that deals in developed properties such as apartments, small stores and professional buildings. Most counselors say that this sort of syndicate is not for the small investor who wants to make his capital grow while sheltering modest current income.

Moreover, this type of syndicate usually demands of its limited partners a certain minimum annual income, usually well above $50,000 a year. Indeed, such a syndicate has little utility for a limited partner who makes less than that.

There is, however, another type of real estate syndicate that often seeks out small investors. That is the *raw land syndicate*. Its function is to leverage a lot of acreage in an area that its promoter feels is going to grow spectacularly within a relatively short period of time and will, as a consequence, "throw off" a sizable capital gain.

This is regarded as the most speculative of all real estate syndicates for two reasons: First, with raw land there is no continuing income, with the exception of agricultural and grazing leases. Everything is outgo—the mortgage amortization, the interest, the property taxes and quite possibly special district assessments too. Second, the liquidity factor is, at best, uncertain since one or two adverse events in an area can soften the raw land market overnight. An airport construction is postponed, a factory decides to locate elsewhere, a vast area is rezoned, etc.

True, there are tax deductions. But there is no depreciation. And it does not take the sort of continuous management that improved property takes. Neither does it take maintenance money. But a raw land syndicate does take something else— continuous research of the most meticulous order.

The promoter of such a syndicate must devote a great deal of time to watching developments in the area. He must be aware of ecological influences and zoning changes. He must watch the tax assessor's office and the sort of transactions that are going on in the area around the syndicate's holdings.

We have seen taxes increase as much as 600 percent on raw range land because a "land butcher" has purchased nearby, hacked up a quarter section into two-and-a-half acre "ranchitos," sold them for twenty times their actual value and disappeared to repeat the process elsewhere.

As soon as the sales are recorded at the new price the assessor's office is alerted. Very soon—particularly in these revenue-hungry days—you may be certain a deputy assessor will be around reappraising the entire area. Such a tax increase can put a raw land syndicate out of business very quickly. Usually it results in an aborted objective or a total loss.

In order to reduce risk, many raw land syndicate operators "churn" the holdings. This means they keep the land for six months, develop a number of prospects who will pay a higher price, dispose of all or part of the original syndicate holdings, and leverage in somewhere else.

A lot of money has been made this way—millions in California, Nevada, Arizona, New Mexico and Utah alone. It is impossible for writers to research them all. But of those examined, either as researchers ,or as possible buyers, it would appear that the promoters are doing somewhat better than the limited partners.

There have been so many abuses—and there have been so many permissive county and state officials in the past whose indifference tacitly encouraged abuses—that the federal government is interesting itself in the operation of most all real estate investment promotions.

Unless a family has solid personal knowledge of a good operator in the real estate syndicate field, it would seem more prudent to choose a less risky land investment with one of the large reputable developers. You may not make a killing. But if you choose your developer wisely, you almost surely will show a profit both in dollars and in peace of mind.

19.
The New "RVRs"

"Get Away," says the attractive color brochure in bold type. "Use your Rec-Vee more frequently. Explore the unspoiled regions of America, breathe clean mountain air, and have the exclusive ownership of your own secluded retreat."

The brochure, presented to us by Outdoor Resorts of America, Inc., of Nashville, Tennessee, is a precursor of a new type of recreational land investment. ORA, Inc., is its principal pioneer. It is a sort of "condominium-on-wheels" concept in which the owner of a recreational vehicle may buy, in fee simple, an improved lot in a motor home park and share an undivided interest in the recreational and service amenities that the developer promises to provide.

The idea has plenty of appeal, particularly to a motor home owner who has driven to one of our national or state parks only to find that all of the spaces have been taken and there may be as much as a two-week wait.

In more and more of our popular vacation areas that are getting to be the rule rather than the exception, the new recreation vehicle industry turns loose on the road each year almost $2 billion in new products. These range from dinky little shoe boxes on wheels that pop up into a "tent" to thirty-two-foot-long luxury motor homes with more living space, appliances and gracious living gadgets than a first-class resort accommodation.

The prospect of all those rolling residences on the road chills the hearts of conservationists and warms the hearts of developers who see new fortunes to be made from the peripatetic American family. Those who just like to go exploring in the family sedan and stop at motels along the way are not always too happy about these new "auto-motivated" adventurers.

Painted on a rock beside Highway 89, just north of Yellowstone National Park, we found the following:

> Breathes there a driver with soul so dead
> Who never to his wife has said,
> "I wish that trailer'd get out the lead,
> Or take the old back road instead!"

Anyone who has fumed along behind an overloaded camper grinding up a tortuous grade can sympathize with those poetic sentiments. But then so can anyone who has been stuck on a two-lane mountain grade behind a laboring parade of splay-wheeled foreign minibuses. So why malign the good old American family that buys a camper or motor home and prays together that it will get a chance to play together out where the buffalo roam and the clouds are not smoggy all day?

Unless we reach the point where a federal bureaucracy begins issuing gas stamps, camping-space tickets and telling us the month of the year and the number of days we may vacation in our first, second or third choice national park or public campground, it is going to be well-nigh impossible to deter a family from taking to the open road.

How much more sensible it is then to provide these happy wanderers with picturesque, clean, well-designed motor home resorts than to force them to crowd into "Campground No. 55" in Yosemite National Park* to enjoy the grandeur of one of the true wonders of the world, parked a scant foot from their neighbor; not to mention having to queue up in the morning chill to use the lavatory.

And how much better it may be to provide a well-planned, well-managed vacation place that our mobile Americans are certain to get into because they *own* ample space in it.

The "land butcher" who plats a "city" in the heart of West Hellangone provides no service. On the contrary, as we shall see in a later chapter, he may be committing an enormous disservice. But (and this is purely a personal opinion based on inspection of a half dozen of these new RV resorts) the developer who delivers on his promise is not only giving the local economy a boost while making a commendable contribution to conservation through good planning, but is also providing a much needed service. We believe that, with one important qualification, he will be accomplishing these objectives *if he is not greedy and does not carve out the maximum number of minisized "pads";* if all of the utilities and services, with emphasis on water supply and waste disposal, are of absolutely top quality and more than adequate capacity; and if first-class maintenance is provided.

In the best of these new RV resorts—those that meet the criteria outlined—buyers will most likely find they have made a sound investment. First of all, unlike those who have been sold a private preserve of Gila monsters and sidewinders out along the "hinges of hell," the owner of a lot in one of the best quality RV resorts will be able to use and enjoy his purchase because all of the subsidiary services he needs are in and working. Also, most all of these RV resorts are located near prime national or state parks.

Another feature in the condominium concept now being developed by Outdoor Resorts of America and other pioneers in

---

*The park authorities are seriously considering limiting the number of people who may camp in any given year.

this new investment field is that, during the time owners are not using their spaces, the resort management will be able to rent them out to carefully selected transient RV owners. This will help to defray part of the purchase price and ongoing association expenses.

To give the reader some idea of what may be involved in such an investment, we visited an ORA development on Long Key, Florida. As platted when we saw it (under construction) in November of 1972, Long Key contained approximately 390 lots of various sizes, the smallest of which seemed to be about 35 x 70 feet.

The development faces on Florida Bay to the north and on the Overseas Highway to the south. Lots nearest the highway were priced in the $6,000 bracket. Those nearer to the water were in the $7,000 to $8,000 bracket. Those facing on the canals cut in from the bay were in the $9,000 price range, and those facing on the bay were in the $10,000 range.

At the time of inquiry, condominium fees were between $15 and $20 a month to cover management and maintenance of the resort and its recreational and service facilities and grounds.

At Long Key, facilities included an administration building and clubhouse, bathhouses for those who wished to ocean-bathe or use the large filtered pool, tennis courts, shuffleboard courts, a putting green, visitor parking space and trailer storage space. Taxes, we were told, were running about $3 to $4 a month, or $36 to $48 a year. No permanently located mobile *homes* are allowed; only motor home recreational vehicles, trailers and campers are permitted in the park.

Outdoor Resorts of America, Inc., is also underway with "Rec-Vee" resorts near Disney World at Orlando, Florida; at Key West; at Nettles Island, north of Palm Beach, very near Stuart, on Florida's Atlantic coast; and in the Smoky Mountains eleven miles east of Gatlinburg, Tennessee, on Highway 73. Management told us that as of February 1, 1973, more Ree-Vee Resorts are planned or under construction at Lake of the

Ozarks, Lake Tahoe and Las Vegas. Others are planned in California, Arizona and Michigan. One is also scheduled to be built in Mexico.

At least a dozen other developers, including two major oil companies, are said to be in, or are about to enter, this new recreation service field. Since the initial investment in such a resort—if it is to be top quality—is in excess of $2 million in "front money," it is hoped that the expense of good development will keep the marginal promoters who work on a leveraged "shoestring" from grabbing up desirable properties and exploiting them.

In Washington, D.C., we were told that "Nader's Raiders" have this new type of development high on their priority list for investigation. So has the Sierra Club and other conservation groups. So perhaps where negligent local authorities fail to keep up standards, public opinion, motivated by the conservationists, will. Aside from the unanchored, bulldozed "cabin" developments that boast nothing but dirt roads and corner stakes festooned with garish plastic streamers, we can think of nothing more dreadful than a lot of beautiful seashore and mountain vacation areas dotted with cheap motor home developments without proper water, power and waste disposal facilities.

A number of large recreation second-home developers, taking a cue from ORA and others, have set aside areas for their own RV parks. These developments will offer a mix of shelter. Permanently sited homes of a minimum square footage will share developed facilities with permanently "blocked" mobile home "coaches" and RV "pads" fully developed to provide power, water, gas and waste disposal. In most of these multiple-use, second-home recreational developments, all owners may enjoy the common club facilities for the payment of an association fee.

In the spring of 1972 we had ample evidence of the wisdom of staking a claim in one of these well-run private developments. In public campgrounds in seven Western states we heard tales of, or saw evidence of, vandalism and violence perpetrated by gangs of young people who came to swim and boat and smoke pot. Many simply came for the "kicks" they could get out of disturbing families who had sought the peace and quiet of the out-of-doors.

We talked to a deputy sheriff at a northern California "lake" that is really part of a huge irrigation system. This patient but harassed man who must try to patrol a 200 square mile area by himself told us that he dreads the weekends and the summer vacation periods.

"It's only the end of June. School hasn't been out two weeks yet. But I've made thirty-five arrests for vandalism, disturbing the peace, armed robbery and illegal use of drugs.

"This may be paradise for some people but it sure is hell for me! The county's got to get more deputies out here. Some of these young hombres are tough, especially if they're "on" something. Drugs. A couple of times I've come close to using my gun—which I sure as hell don't want to do unless I have to."

In this same public campground we saw trash cans turned over, obscene grafitti sprayed on rest rooms and a service buildings, boats vandalized at their floats, others cut adrift at their moorings during the night, outboard motors stolen, gas tanks wantonly destroyed, swimming beaches made filthy with human excrement, swimming pools littered with soft drink cans, liquor bottles and food cartons and the remnants of picnic lunches strewn all over the place despite numerous trash cans within easy reach.

"Some of these people—mostly young people—are just plain onry [sic] pigs," said the manager of one leased marina and campground. "As a taxpayer I resent like anything having to pay more and more money to hire help to clean up after them.

"The wife and I thought this would be an ideal life for us when I retired. But we're getting out of here the end of summer. We can't take it anymore. It's getting downright dangerous now. You ask a teenage punk not to throw his trash around and like as not he'll throw it in your face. If you try to do anything about it, you could get a knife in your belly! To hell with that!"

When we asked this worried man where he and his wife would go, he replied, "To one of the private trailer parks. I've got an offer to manage one. At least there we can control who comes in."

The problems this worried man and his wife told us about could very well become the most persuasive argument a salesman for the new RV resorts could use. We are convinced from personal inspection that the problems are not exaggerated.

What kind of a family investment would a lot in a well-situated, well-designed and well-managed RV resort be? A very promising one, or so it would appear from the statistics.

For instance, the total number of campsites, both public and private, has increased less than 10 percent a year in the past two years. But manufacturers of recreation vehicles reported production of 525,000 units during 1971—up 11 percent over 1970. The biggest gain was in motor homes—57,200 units, up from 30,300 *a gain of 89 percent over the previous year!*

The largest numerical gain was in travel trailers—181,000, up from 138,000—a gain of 32 percent. Camping trailers and pickup covers were down.

With some 4 million units on our roads it does not take much imagination to see the size of the market. Some indication of the wealth of the market may be gained from the weekend sales of one large multiple-lot dealer in Southern California: Four $46,000 thirty-foot motor homes, nine smaller ones in the $20,000 price range and eleven in the $10,000 class.

The result of this increase in recreation vehicle traffic has been to raise the entrance fees in state and federal recreational areas. At some destinations such as Yosemite, Yellowstone and Great Smoky, it is a case of "no room at the inn" for weeks on end. There are hundreds of turn-aways each summer, and in some areas reservations are now required. Just outside the boundaries of Grand Teton Park which no longer permits over-flow camping, there are 1,350 private campsites, mostly operated on a per night basis.

By the summer of 1971, private developments had provided almost double the number of RV sites the public facilities were able to furnish. The gap has been closing somewhat during the past year, but it is important to note that, in quality, many public facilities must be regarded as primitive when compared with the best of the privately financed RV resorts.

The principal advantages enjoyed by owners and renters of lots in the private RV resorts are large sites instead of the minimum spaces or pads. Water, electricity and sewer facilities are available at each lot. Available also are clubhouses, recreational amenities such as swimming pools, planned beach areas, tennis and shuffleboard courts, horseshoe rinks, volleyball courts, archery ranges and, in some parks, king-size checkerboards and chessboards. Of utmost importance to those who have deserted the public facilities, there is the security of supervised access on a twenty-four-hour basis.

These days there is seldom a "green light" for any kind of development, even if it is well done and provides a recognized service. So it is not surprising to find a government study group proposing a tax on capital gains derived from "land speculations" (a very general definition that may be hard to pinpoint) plus a tax on recreation vehicles. Money from the proposed taxes would be used to finance a *$100 billion* federal urban park land acquisition and development program. The study group also advocates a moratorium on road building and the installation of parking lots in national parks to reduce car traffic. In their place, the group would encourage camping rather than recreation-vehicle living.

There is no way to predict what the outcome of such a plan will be. When questioned about the idea one Park Service ranger smiled tolerantly and said, "Let's just hope they study real hard back there in Washington. If they do they might discover that few things are cleaner and better organized than a good recreation vehicle, and few things are messier than a bunch of amateur campers. Already we're back-packing their litter down from the highest peaks in the United States. And maybe if those professors study *real* hard they'll also discover that campers have to drive to their campsites in automobiles. We get very few horses and buggies anymore!"

Another Park Service official was more direct:

"The last thing in the world the government needs now is more public land. We own better than 50 percent of several states now. What we need are more national parks, the personnel to operate them properly, and a public relations campaign to attract people to them—away from the overcrowded spots. But that has become a political football too. Every time we suggest that the solution is more national parks, the environmentalists start yelling again. We're caught in a real bind. We've got the money to provide more vacation places, but the politicians are afraid to let us spend it."

Many organizations, including the National Campground Owners Association in Delray Beach, Florida, feel the recreation vehicle industry is on the threshold of a spectacular boom. A number of indicators point in the direction of a huge upsurge in the ownership of RV lots, undivided interests and the club concept in general. The industry is paying particular attention to a California developer, N. E. Isaacson, and his "Snowflower" project—a 670-acre membership campground in the historic Donner Pass area of the Sierra Nevada.

Located in a well-timbered 5,700-foot-high mountain valley complete with an Alpine stream and a sizable lake, the location seems ideal. "Snowflower" is situated within a mile or so of U.S. Interstate 80, the main freeway over the Sierra Range to Nevada and its Reno and Tahoe gaming clubs. Sixty miles from the California State capital at Sacramento and 145 miles from San Francisco, the RV resort is within easy driving distance of population centers totaling more than 2 million people, most of whom have long been mountain-orientated.

The so-called amenity package is regarded as exceptional by professionals in the campground development industry; and all of this "conserved beauty" and planned convenience is available to members for around $3,000. Little wonder that "Snow-flower" is being watched with much interest nationally since it may provide still another way in which we mobile Americans can enjoy the blessings of nature for a relatively modest price.

A great many of the 4 million families who owned recreation vehicles as of 1972 may soon expect to receive a barrage of direct-mail advertising offering them ownership of RVR lots or memberships or undivided interests.

The secret of effective direct-mail selling is a good prospect list. The recreation industry is especially favored with such lists that will enable them to zero in on bona fide prospects instead of using the "shotgun" technique that most direct-mail offerings depend on.

RVR promoters feel that one of the ways to keep quality development costs down and prices within reach of an average family is to keep sales costs down. The recreational vehicle owner who loves his motor home or travel trailer and uses it at every opportunity, despite the crowding at his favorite beach, desert or mountain vacation area, becomes a prime prospect for ownership in a RV resort since he is "100 percent sold" on that way of life to start with. So if you own an RV, look carefully at the "junk mail." Not all of it may be junk.

There is one other type of development, just beginning to be pioneered in California by North American Towns of California, that does not fit squarely into either the recreational second-home category or the new own-your-own recreational vehicle resort. No generic name has yet been devised for it though we have no doubt that developer N. K. Mendelsohn, who also heads Fort Clark Springs in Texas, will come up with one.

Called *Battle Creek Ranches,* this new recreational concept occupies some 26,700 acres of land on the east side of the Sacramento River in Shasta County. The concept is new. Not all of it had been finally approved at the time we visited the area in February of 1973. Bounded by Battle Creek on the south and by the Lassen National Park Highway on the north, the huge expanse of heavily wooded and open meadowland extends from the Sacramento River roughly eleven miles eastward to within easy driving distance of the famous volcanic national park and its all-year recreational areas.

The trees and shrubs are mainly oak, "digger" pine, cottonwood, manzanita, and willow thickets along the streams. The western boundary of Battle Creek Ranches touches a stretch of the river that is famed for its salmon and bass. The half-dozen perennial creeks on the property are well stocked with rainbow and Eastern brook trout, and wild game abounds. Indian artifacts are often found by hunters and fishermen, and for many years the Bear Creek petroglyphs have fascinated students of American Indian lore.

North American Towns of California has committed 24,500 acres to ranches of approximately 48 acres each. Properly, these are "recreational ranches." Buyers become members of a club and the Battle Creek Park Association composed entirely of owners of these 48-acre parcels. Members will operate four so-called common areas of approximately 440 acres on which will be built recreational amenities. An assessment of $180 per year is contemplated for the maintenance of the facilities or for such additional installations as the members may desire in the future.

In their correspondence explaining the plan, North American Towns say, "Recorded Protective Covenants assure property owners and members of the continuous availability of adequate assessments to support and expand the facilities on the common recreational areas as well as to maintain 'private roads' which we are constructing. Incidentally, these 'private roads' are built to Shasta County standards. . . ."

Shasta County, well aware of what has happened elsewhere, set a precedent by establishing standards for private roads that the county will not maintain. Owners who pay assessments for the maintenance of their roads may take some comfort from the fact that well-engineered roads require less care than the usual roughed-out "ranch roads" that provide access to most open land.

The plan for Battle Creek Ranches contrasts with the Fort Clark Springs concept in that the Texas development *sells* a membership and an undivided interest with the provision that each member can acquire title to his own separate building site when, as and if he is ready to build. A Battle Creek Ranch owner receives a membership automatically with his purchase. Obviously then, in the Battle Creek offering, North American Towns of California is aiming for a substantially higher income group.

Closer to the Fort Clark Springs concept will be a segment of the property presently designated as Battle Creek Recreational Park. Two thousand acres, part of which borders on the east bank of the Sacramento River, will be maintained as one undivided parcel. As presently planned, about 3,000 undivided interests will be created. These may also be termed "memberships." This aspect of the development is designed to appeal to owners of recreational vehicles or others who just wish to enjoy the area in their private cars. The developer plans a number of amenities including boat-launching facilities which, at some point, will be taken over and administered by a body that may be called the Battle Creek Recreation Association. At present each of these memberships is being tentatively priced at $1,990 to put them within reach of modest investors. North American Towns of California says that it does not presently plan to provide separate lot ownerships as a part of the membership, as in Fort Clark Springs. However, the possibility is not ruled out according to N. K. Mendelsohn.

Because of the size of the holding and its nature, the developer contemplates an interesting income possibility for individual owners. Long a splendid cattle-grazing area, the officials feel that the pro rata share of winter grazing leases should produce about one dollar an acre—about enough to cover the road maintenance burden.

At the time we visited this interesting new concept, sales had not begun. Roads were being engineered and parcels surveyed, and preliminary work was underway on the installation of utilities and other amenities in the public areas.

One thing seems certain: if North American Towns is successful in selling out its 48-acre ranches, each owner will have access to the family property over excellent roads, and certainly nobody will be right smack up against anybody else. It is big country, and a very beautiful one. The entire area will be posted to protect the indigenous wild game; and with two fish hatcheries nearby, it seems unlikely that even an incompetent angler will get skunked in the well-stocked streams.

Battle Creek Ranches is reached through the historic little town of Cottonwood, just off Interstate 5 north of Red Bluff. With the advent of the development some changes have come over the sleepy little town. The developer had his designers draw up a concept of how the frontier aspect of Cottonwood could be restored. Then he went to the local businessmen with a proposition: "I'll supply the plans and the paint if you fellows want to spruce up Main Street!"

The transformation is remarkable, and so is the infusion of "civic pride" that accompanied it! It is not a coincidence, however, that North American Towns of California maintains its headquarters in a row of old buildings that it purchased. As much as anything, the example the developer set got the other owners to "sprucing things up." Battle Creek Ranches is a new concept, and it is being carefully watched by all levels of government and by the development industry as well.

20.
The High-Pressure Pitch

"Hi there! My name is Maggie." The attractive young lady, whose Kelly-green miniskirt displayed a perfectly turned pair of legs clad in sheer black pantyhose, thrust a clutch of folders at us so insistently that we took them in self-defense. "Welcome to The Golden Fleece Club!* Is this your first time in Las Vegas?"

Some intuitive perversity made us both nod in the affirmative even though we had been in Las Vegas several times during the past few years.

"You'll love it here," enthused Maggie. "It's neat!" Before we could add, "but gawdy," she continued. "I represent the chamber of commerce and I also act as hostess for the Honest Acres Land Company. We want you to be our guests for one of the big casino shows and get to know Las Vegas . . . and also the fabulous new city we are building." She glanced around quickly then added in a confidential whisper, "It may be the only safe thing in town to put your money in!"

---

*Names of casinos, developments and personnel are fictitious, but be assured that events reported herein were real enough.

We chuckled conspiratorially and allowed ourselves to be led to a garishly decorated booth in the lobby where three more very attractive young women in abbreviated Robin Hood outfits turned on magical smiles as we approached. Each handed us a prepared packet of literature and Maggie, making it clear that we were "special people," explained quietly to the bosomy blonde "mother superior" of the front crew that we were the "neatest couple" she'd met all evening.

From somewhere a very mod young man appeared. He had the dark, hirsute good looks of those faceless young leading men who shine for thirteen weeks in a television cop-and-robber series and are seldom heard from again. His smile was dazzling, his handshake firm and his manner earnest as he proffered two forms to be filled out.

"These are chamber of commerce forms. The information is fed into a computor to help us learn what visitors to Las Vegas want most," he explained. We were tempted to reply that what visitors to Vegas wanted most was a chance to win once in a while, but we resisted and dutifully filled out the forms: Name, address, phone, age, occupation, number of dependents; make of car, state registered, paid for or financed; bank accounts, credit cards; home owned or rented, other property, description and location of same; clubs belong to, reason for visiting Las Vegas, and other incidentals that we do not recall.

Since the information was no more than that usually requested by a department store when a credit account is opened, we filled in the blanks, signed and returned the forms to our leading man. He assured us that the chamber of commerce would be grateful.

Maggie pointed to theatrical-type tickets in our packets. "Fill out the spaces, Mr. and Mrs. Cooley, and put the stubs in the bowl. We are going to have a drawing in fifteen minutes and you may win a prize."

Again we obeyed and Maggie winked winningly and murmured, "Good luck." It was the young leading man's turn again.

"Incidentally, my name is Rick. Mind if I call you by your first name, Leland?"

"Heck no," replied the graying male half of this team in his best "yokelized" drawl, "all the kids on the block do." The put-on was obvious but the young man managed a laugh and a coy, comradely shoulder punch across the counter. "Love a man with a sense of humor! Most older people get a little uptight about filling in our chamber of commerce forms. They don't understand it's for their own good." Rick's forced smile dissolved into a look of thoughtful concern.

"Now Leland—and Lee—I'll tell you what I'd like you to do. I'd like you to be our guests for breakfast and our preview reception in the morning and see a show of your choice tomorrow evening. We will show you a fifteen-minute color film of the fantastic Hasarai Valley which will explain why our new city of Lago Seco is destined to become the third largest in the state."

Lowering his voice, despite the fact that a half dozen other "exceptional couples" were bunched around us, he said, "I've been in the land development game all of my life, and this is the most incredible opportunity I've ever seen. My wife and I own there, and we're counting on the profit from our lot to put our kids through college." He glanced at the information form again. "I see you already own property, but I want you to see the film anyway. Obviously you know about land investment, and I'd like you to tell me whether you think we made a wise investment."

We concealed our amusement and agreed to see the film at eight the following morning, after a complimentary breakfast. The young man's sales psychology was straight out of the land hustler's manual, "If the prospects are older, ask their opinion of the purchase you have made for your family in the development. Nine out of ten people will be kind and agree that it is good. When they do, you have begun to condition them subjectively to the idea that our deal may be a good investment for them too."

We reassured him and Maggie moved between us and took us by the arms with convincing affection. "Have fun now and I'll see you in the morning. You two are 'neat'!"

We were not interested in the shows or the prizes, but we were definitely interested in the development and in the present state of the art of high-pressure land selling. We wandered around the casino making minor investments until about ten o'clock, then went to our room, weary after a difficult drive from Phoenix in a sleet storm.

At 6:45 the next morning Maggie called, bright as ever, to make certain we didn't miss the free breakfast at 7:30.

We dressed and scurried through still more sleet to the casino breakfast room where we were asked to show our credentials. "A lot of freeloaders try to chisel a breakfast," we were told. Then we were steered to a booth, served the Sixty-Five Cent Special—one cold scrambled egg, a fossilized link sausage and a dab of hash brown potatoes still frozen in the center. (The orange juice was a dollar extra—fifty cents each—we discovered.) The waitress looked so harassed we left her a generous tip and rushed to the reception.

At the door of the meeting room we found our young hero again clutching the sheaf of chamber of commerce forms. This time he was lining up the sheep for alphabetical shearing—two to a "shearer." When our name was called, he handed the sheet to a "salesman" waiting at the door, introduced us and all but pushed us in.

As we followed the "salesman" to a table for three, complete with contract forms, pens and plastic coffee cups, we saw him scanning the material. When he came to the line marked "occupation" we heard him mutter, very distinctly, "Sh——!"

From the moment we were seated it was apparent that our "corporate representative"—the usual euphemism for a salesman without a license—was very unhappy. In fact, he was hardly civil.

The lights dimmed, the screen lit up with a corporate insignia that made the great seal of the United States of America look like a Cracker Jack prize, and we began listening to a very able pitchman. For twenty minutes he told us about land in general and about the multi-million dollar corporation that was founded by a group of sterling men whose one aim in life was to make us rich.

We heard all of the usual clichés—George Washington, Benjamin Franklin and Andrew Carnegie all had personally recommended land investment as the only sure way to make a fortune. And we heard again the truism: "Every year we're making more people but we aren't making more land." (Fine! But that does not imply urgent buyer demand everywhere, especially not in the middle of "West Hellangone.")

The pitchman was real talent. He had the charisma and articulateness of a Billy Graham or an Oral Roberts, but we got the impression that an abyss lay between these evangelists where principles were concerned.

While this was going on, we could sense our corporate representative alternately studying the chamber of commerce form and us. When at last the pitch ended and the proposed miracle had been illustrated with an artist's blown-up renditions of civic centers, equestrian centers, shopping malls, schools, churches, parks, bicycle paths, recreation centers, family clubs, swimming pools and all of the other standard accessories, the lights came on and we found a filled-in contract had been unobtrusively positioned for signing.

Despite the fact that the platted city of Lago Seco, situated only an hour from almost anywhere, could theoretically accommodate nearly a quarter of a million residents, we were told that the choice lots were "going fast."

"What you'd better do, Cooley," advised the corporate representative gruffly, "is give me a check for five hundred dollars now, and I'll reserve this lot for you." He had "exed" a corner lot priced at fifty-five hundred dollars.

"The five hundred dollars will be put in a savings account in your name. You've got three months to make up your mind. If you decide that you don't want the property after you've seen it, you'll get every penny of your five hundred dollars back. How can you lose?"

"What about the interest?" we asked.

The question produced an incredulous stare that melted to a look of pity. *"We* keep that, of course! We're entitled to something." After another close inspection of the information form he looked up accusingly. "You filled this thing out truthfully, didn't you? You've got five hundred bucks, haven't you?"

Struggling against a mounting desire to recite the scriptures according to Dale Carnegie, the male half of this collaboration shook his head. "Nope. Not on me."

The "salesman's" face reddened with frustration. "I don't mean 'on you'! I mean in the bank."

"Yes, I have five hundred bucks in the bank."

"Well then, write me a check and let's get this deal closed. You saw the presentation. You know what an opportunity it is. If you're worried about the twelve dollars and fifty cents in interest, hell, we'll deduct that from the first month's payment."

"What payment? We haven't heard about that."

"Look, Cooley, the monthly payments on your lot are fifty-two bucks. It says right here in the contract that you have to pay them for three months while you're making up your mind."

"Your friend up there at the podium didn't say anything about that."

"Of course not, he doesn't talk dollars. That's my job. That's what I'm here for—to give you personal attention."

"Does that include answering our questions?"

"If they make sense, sure."

"Does it make any sense for us to ask what happens to the one hundred and fifty six dollars in payments—if we decide we don't want the land?"

"You don't have to worry about that," he said. "And I'll tell you why. When you see the land, you are not only going to thank me for selling it to you but you are going to beg me to sell you more!"

"Well, that may very well be. Those artist's renditions look very promising. But we never buy land without actually seeing it first, so this is what we'll do. Tomorrow, on the way home, we'll detour over to the Hasarai Valley and look at the land. If we like what we see, we'll get in touch with you and talk some more."

The corporate representative pushed his chair back angrily and got up. "You can't do that!"

"Why not, for heaven's sake?" asked the female half.

"Because if you do, the salesman on the property gets you and he gets credit for the sale. That's not fair!"

"You mean we have to buy the property first, before we can go down to see it?"

Exasperated, the "salesman" said a bit too loudly, "You two sure ask a lot of questions! Of course you don't have to buy it. You just give me a check for five hundred dollars to *reserve* it. That way I get the credit—"

"And the commission—we understand that. But I'll tell you what, Mr.———, we own some good land around the country and we've never bought an acre of it without first looking it over very carefully. And we also like to know as much as possible about the people who are selling it." At this point we rose. "So, we'll just drop in, look the place over, and if the on-site salesman approaches us, we'll explain that we are your prospects. And that is the only way we'll do it."

As we made our move to leave, a voice in the back of the room shouted, "Folks, congratulate Mr. and Mrs. Clyde Frannis of Omak, Washington, for being the first lucky couple to buy a lot in Lago Seco today! Let's give them a big hand." Waving a check for all to see, he beckoned the smiling shills to rise while he led the applause provided mainly by the dozen or so corporate representatives at the other tables.

We paused in the aisle and found ourselves confronted by our young leading man, Rick, who finally identified himself as the area sales manager. Standing beside him, very unhappy at the couple he'd drawn, was our representative.

"These people had no intention of buying anything when they came in," he charged, shoving the chamber of commerce form at Rick. "They're writers! And you remember what happened the last time, don't you?"

Rick nodded tolerantly. "Sure, but that guy represented himself as a plumber from Chicago and he introduced the dame as his wife, which she wasn't. I'm sure the Cooleys—"

"That's right!" cut in the corp-rep. "They were no more married than you and I are. They were reporters. Two weeks after they were here we got ripped apart in a New York paper. So why did this guy take a million notes during the film pitch?"

At this point the male half's faded merchant marine tattoo began to itch—a danger sign which young Rick read correctly. Taking us by the arms he herded us gently outside.

"Let me just ask you one thing—are you reporters?"

"No," we answered. "We are precisely what we represented ourselves to be on *your* chamber of commerce forms— professional writers. We write books."

"Well, may I ask you another question: Are you interested in buying a lot at Lago Seco?"

"We can't answer that until we've seen the place. So far all we have seen is an artist's rendition of *proposed* improvements. We have heard no hard facts that would lead us to believe there's any reason for building the state's third largest city in the Hasarai Valley."

Rick listened, nodding and smiling. Then he stuck out his hand and said, "You're free to go now, folks—without the show tickets or premiums, of course—because you didn't sign up for them last night. Personally, I think you're making a big mistake. And when things really get rolling out there next year I'm going to give you a call and prove it to you."

We replied that it was risk we were going to have to take, said brief farewells, and went over to a row of slot machines from which vantage point we could watch the other exceptional couples make their exits from the pressure cooker.

We talked to four couples in the casino afterward. None had bought. None had been given their show tickets because they had neglected to sign up for them the night before—a fine point that somehow seemed not to have been made entirely clear. Later we saw the lucky couple who had bought the first lot, return and take their places in the back of the room—all of which may lend a special significance to that old Latin injunction, "Caveat emptor."

We do not think that we would have gained anything by not identifying ourselves as writers. If the corp-rep had been a professional salesman, he would have picked up on "writer" and would have immediately begun asking us some discreet questions about our profession. In that case we would have told him that the male half writes novels, three of which have sold to pictures, and that together we write nonfiction works, among them books on retirement and land investment. And we would have hastened to add that we also invest in land regularly when we find situations where the indicators show promise of reasonable growth and development.

There is a vast difference between owning acreage in the Antelope Valley and owning a building lot in the Hasarai Valley—or in any of the other remote "Hasarai Valleys" where unanchored subdivisions are platted, not for the purpose of building a Reston or a Columbia, but for the purpose of making the promoters an outrageous profit on cheap raw land.

We know that one developer bought several thousand acres in a little valley for $10 an acre in 1955. Ten years later the developer sold the land to an eastern firm for $150 an acre. In the intervening decade no improvement of any great consequence had been added. Alfalfa grows there and some cotton. And there seems to be a good water table. But there are no other indicators to show the need for a city there now, or in the foreseeable future. But raw land within a twenty-five-mile radius of any growing city, on or near a main road, could well be another kind of investment, as the records will show.

The "pressure-cooker" sales technique is the crudest and the cruelest of all. We have seen older people leave one of those receptions literally ill from the rousting they get from these unlicensed corporate representatives, or vice-presidents, or land counselors—or strong-arm men by any other name.

The ones that operate in Las Vegas and Reno are usually wooing California residents who come across the state line to gamble. The companies have either chosen not to sell in California because of the state's stringent out-of-state land sales laws (the strongest in the nation, with the possible exception of New York), or they have not been able to qualify. Nevada state officials have received many complaints from out-of-state visitors who enjoy the games and the shows but who have had their pleasure, and often their purses, seriously diminished by the roughshod treatment accorded them by land hustlers.

It would be doing an injustice to some, however, to say that all casino receptions are "pressure-cooker" operations. In Reno, quite by accident, we encountered one as we entered a major casino on Virginia Street.

The developer was promoting a huge new city on the west coast of Florida called Rotonda West. Occupying some 26,000 acres of the old Vanderbilt estate, it is roughly ten miles as the crow flies from the successful developments of Port Charlotte and Punta Gorda. The exclusive community of Cape Haze adjoins Rotonda on the west.

The vice-president in charge of community relations is Ed McMahon, Johnny Carson's long-time sidekick on "The Tonight Show." The developer is the Cavanaugh Communities Corporation.

The reception and presentation we attended was a masterpiece of showmanship and low-key sell. True, the sales crew offered inducements such as a free roll of nickels for the slots if we would just stop and talk, and ten silver dollars if we would attend the sales presentation. We stopped, looked and listened, and received both. And we also received the impression that if the Cavanaugh Communities Corporation is able to complete its plans and see its development dream come true, they will surely have created one of the most unusual communities in Florida or anywhere else.

In May of 1972, work was going ahead on the facilities the developer promised to undertake, some of it to be completed by 1977. A box beneath the panoramic depiction of the completed development shown in the handsome presentation brochure reads:

> This is a true architect's rendering of Rotonda West—improvements shown do not exist. Improvements promised are limited to paved streets, recreational canals, drainage systems, water and sewerage facilities, marinas, golf courses clubhouses, which are scheduled for completion by December 31, 1977. Construction of residential and commercial buildings is not the responsibility of the developer. They are merely shown for the purpose of depicting the zoning of the development.

A fair enough statement, it would seem, and compared to some of the promises we've heard (usually not committed to paper) it would also seem to be a model of forthrightness. Rotonda West is an exciting dream, one that you can't help but wish will turn out, providing the ecological considerations have been given as much professional attention as all else seems to have received.

At no time were we pressured. We asked and got straight answers to our questions. The salesman, an affable old pro who sized us up correctly in a few minutes of talk, said, "Mr. and Mrs. Cooley, I've enjoyed meeting you but I do not think I'm going to have the pleasure of signing you up today. Not many people who come in here ask the kind of questions you do, though we wish they would. I know you've got the money to buy if you want to so I'm going to suggest this: You pay your own transportation to Rotonda and back, and we'll pay all of your other expenses for five days and four nights. You'll be our guests—nothing to pay except maybe some bar and restaurant tips if you want to. The offer holds good except on weekends and during the heart of the winter season. If you'll go down and look at Rotonda, I'll bet that you'll come back here and buy. How about that? Fair?"

"Fair enough," we agreed, and said if the opportunity presented itself we would drive over and see the development.

In November of 1972 we flew to Miami to begin a national radio and television promotion tour on our new book *How to Avoid the Retirement Trap* that eventually took us to eighteen cities. We decided to steal a day off and drive across the state to visit Rotonda.

On Sunday we rented a car and started out in a thunderstorm that was straight out of the Old Testament. Halfway across the Tamiami Trail, the air-conditioning stopped functioning. Sweltering, we made it to the outskirts of Naples where the windshield wipers quit. From the radio which managed to work throughout, we learned that Miami was experiencing an unseasonal tropical storm that threatened to become a hurricane. And we were due to head back into it.

A service station operator tried for an hour to fix the electrical windshield wipers without success. We called the Naples office of the nationwide car rental service to see if their people could fix the wipers and air-conditioner, or exchange the car for one that would work.

The young lady explained that no mechanics were available on the Sabbath and that no cars were available because they were in the midst of changing to '73 models which had not arrived as yet and all the '72s were no longer okay for rental. We believed her! It occurred to us that a competitive car rental outfit might "try harder," but they had no cars. (We were just going to leave the junk heap in Naples.)

Fifty-nine more miles north on Highway 41 was Punta Gorda. And it would take another ten or fifteen miles of driving to get to Rotonda. Reluctantly, we gave up since we were due to fly to Washington at midnight and we had to get back to the Fountainbleau in Miami Beach to pack.

It was a good thing we did give up. We crawled back through one hundred and thirty miles of sheeting downpour and a barrage of blinding lightening bolts that often struck within a hundred feet of us. Dozens of cars simply stopped to wait out the storm. We should have, too, but we didn't want to miss our flight.

We love Florida. But like California, it can have its moments. Also, like California, before the state got tough about sub-divisions, Florida has had other troubles such as those with the high-pressure promoters who have whacked up undrained swamp and sold it for up to fifty times what the land cost.

On the other hand, we can remember ten years ago when we visited Port Charlotte and Port St. Lucie and were told by local seers that General Development Corporation was certainly out to "swindle the suckers."

General Development has grown into one of the largest and most respected community development organizations in the country, and on a recent visit to the two "Port" cities we talked with "early settlers" who were very happy they had purchased there. Not only have the developments grown into viable com-munities, but the owners' original investments had increased very substantially.

One can always scout up a few malcontents. We had them in our condominium in New York City, and it was regarded as one of the best on Manhattan Island. We meet them in Laguna Beach where we live part-time, and it would be hard to find a more beautiful and better run small (12,000) community any-where in the world.

It is human nature to "view with alarm." The barstool doomsday sayers know that, generally speaking, "good news is not news," so they protect their reputations as "I-Told-You-So-And-Sos" by betting negatively, seldom aware that in the end they are betting against themselves.

Even when the product is good, land salesmen find it difficult to resist the proved performance of some old sales ploys. Most of our readers will have encountered them at one time or another. But a surprising number of "victims" are really not aware of what is happening to them, that is, how the salesman is

imbuing them with a sense of urgency to make a decision
to buy.

Following are five of the most common gimmicks.

The Pushpin Gambit

When you enter the sales office of any sizable subdivision
development, one of the first things you'll see after the salesman's winning smile, is a great map or plat of the subdivision. It
will usually be done in striking colors, and sometimes there will
be dimensional drawings of headquarters building with an arrow
and a sign reading, "You Are Here."

The whole development will usually be divided into units—
Unit 1, Unit 2, and so on. Each will be given a distinctive color
key and a pleasant or distinguished-sounding name—subjective
"value builders."

Each of these units will be divided into lots and now, in the
days of ecological awareness, green belts or open space. These
lots will be classified as single-family residence, multiple,
business, and so on.

And in most of the lots, despite the fact that the development may be only a month old, there will be colorful pushpins:
red for "sold," yellow for "reserved," and green for "open." In
some instances open lots will not be impaled.

After you have been given the "birds-eye view" of the development and some provocative facts and figures—with perhaps a
distinguished name dropped here and there of smart, wealthy
people who have bought or reserved—you will be taken on a
tour.

In the company Wagonaire or Travel-all you will visit the
points of interest: the recreational amenities, completed or
under construction, the homes being built and, finally, the lots
that are still available in Unit 1 or the lots under construction
that will soon be available in Unit 2.

A salesman who knows how to "program" his tour will have
kindled your interest in the "value builders" that the developer

is designing into the project and for which he is "paying." He also will have shown you lots that have increased in value since the owners bought them because they are located closest to the clubhouse complex or the first tee of the golf course.

There will be one particular lot that "a doctor" just bought, a real bargain, and it's a shame you didn't get here last week because it was about a thousand dollars less than comparable lots in the block. But there will be others in Unit 2 that will be just as good and it may be, if you like a particular one, you can get a predevelopment price on it.

After the tour you will be taken back to the office and steered again over to the map filled with pushpins in order to orientate you to what you've seen.

While you're being orientated the sales manager will step up unobtrusively and remove the red pushpin from the doctor's lot and put a green one in its place. Your salesman will feign surprise, excuse himself, intercept the sales manager a few steps away and engage him in earnest conversation. Shaking his head, he will return to the map.

"I can't understand why Dr. Pillheimer let it go! It doesn't make sense."

If you're human, you'll be curious and you'll be told that the sales manager received a call a few minutes ago saying the doctor finds himself unable to go through with the purchase now. "Of course the company will refund his money."

You'll ask about the price if the lot is back on the market and the salesman will ponder a moment, excuse himself again, confer in a nearby office and return, all smiles.

"Jim said if you two are interested, you can have the lot at the same price the doctor paid. I don't want to influence you, but I don't think there will be any more bargains like this one again."

If the development seems promising and if the developer seems likely to keep his promises, you are probably quite interested. In that case the odds are that you'll snap up the bargain. And you'll never know whether or not Dr. Pillheimer was fact or fiction.

Moreover, if you did get a good buy, and you are happy with it, it really doesn't matter. But you should know how it happened to you!

The Two-Way Radio Ploy

This one works best in the big, wide-open-space land subdivisions where several sections are involved. The technique is the same. Only the tools are different.

You'll see the map and the pushpins, or colored crosses marking the sold parcels. And you'll get in the company transport. It is worth saying here that, in general, the shoddier the deal the more elegant the transport. Beware of salesmen who use Cadillacs and Lincolns as "jeeps"! The big corporations don't waste money on such window-dressing. They put you in one of a fleet of serviceable company station wagons or four-wheel drive personnel carriers, each bearing a modest corporate insignia and a fleet unit number. Usually these transports are both heated and air-conditioned, and they may also be equipped with two-way radios for contact with each other and with the sales office.

If the radio ploy is to be used on you—and not all such communications are part of a well-rehearsed "script"—it will probably work like this:

You'll take the tour, and you'll find yourself interested in one or two special parcels of land, either or both of which will be "reserved" or "held on deposit." The salesman will plan your itinerary so that you have passed those two parcels at least twice. Very subtly you will be made to agree that they are exceptionally well located and priced. You will pass them again on your way back to the sales office if, in the meantime, you have not actually expressed interest in another parcel.

During the tour you have probably been dimly aware of the soft, businesslike background chatter of the radio. Unaware that the salesman has sneaked the sound volume up, you will suddenly hear your car being called. The salesman will become alert, excuse himself and pick up the microphone.

"This is car thirteen. Come in."

The office station will come in—usually a pleasant female voice—saying that there has been a change in the Unit One map.

The salesman will pull over, ask your indulgence again, get out the well-worn unit map and a pencil. Then he will reply, "Car thirteen ready to copy." (If he puts it precisely like that, he's probably an ex-Marine Corps or Navy flier!)

At this point a short conversation will ensue, couched in legal descriptive language that will be unintelligible to the prospect but will identify one of the reserved parcels you have seen.

More terse rigamarole will follow, ending with "Car thirteen out." The salesman will mark the map with his pencil and turn to you surprised and excited.

"You know that big corner parcel on the lake that you two liked? The one that was reserved? For some reason that's back on the market."

Without asking your permission he will tool the vehicle around and unless you stop him you'll soon find yourself at the parcel again, quite probably being invited to walk around on it for a closer look. Again, if you are "sold" on the development in general, the odds are that you'll be sold on the lucky parcel too!

There is another variation on the radio ploy that is worth including. In fact, it may now be more common than the one just described. Essentially, you are in the same situation—taking the tour. Suddenly the radio crackles, and the young lady manning the sales office station will call your car. When your driver answers, she will ask if Lot 23 is still on the "open list."

Your driver will check and discover that it is still open for sale. "If you are not showing it, Harry Hustle (another salesman) has a party waiting here to see it," the girl tells him.

By a curious coincidence, Lot 23 is the attractive parcel your salesman has been concentrating on in his low-pressure way. "Tell Harry I'll get back to him. My party is looking at twenty-three now," he responds.

If you have been interested but could not make up your mind because of price, this ploy may help you reach a decision. When you get back to the office to sign the papers and make a deposit, you will find that poor Harry Hustle has been forced to scout up another "exceptional bargain" for his prospects—if, indeed, they existed.

The "I'll Buy It Myself" Hustle

If you have been properly conditioned by a salesman who has not used the pushpin ploy on you yet, or who is not equipped with a two-way radio, you may be persuaded to buy by a simpler, more ingenuous, if not more ingenious, tactic.

This one works best if the salesman is especially young and personable and is possessed of the inborn talent of a high-class confidence man. We have had this method used on us and have been amused by the young man's histrionic ability. We have bought anyway because everything added up, because the salesman did not misrepresent or pressure, and because we liked the young man in question.*

This gambit works best if the young salesman has prosperous "vibes" and is taking you on the tour in his new Jaguar or Mercedes because "all of the company cars are in use now."

You learn from the salesman who is skilled at conveying with becoming modesty that, young as he is, he can hardly believe his good fortune. This month alone he's sold "umpteen" choice parcels. It is clear that even with a modest commission the young man will make in excess of $50,000 for the year. The newly affluent usually make pleasant company and, besides, he has found a way to let you know that, as lucky as he is, beside

---

*Right, Tom?

your material assets he's a piker. "But just give me time! I'm putting as much as I can into land here too!"

This young salesman also has a "special lot" in mind. Before you are really aware of it, he is easing his expensive sedan over roughed-out roads. You protest that he should not abuse his fine car, and he demurs because nothing is too much trouble for such nice people.

You arrive at the lot, find that it is indeed well located (it must be or the ploy is not credible), but you are still a bit hesitant. The salesman does not attempt to rush you. He may even suggest that you get back in the car to look at some other property that is still "good but a little less expensive."

Then, when he senses the timing is right, he will tell you confidentially that he is not really trying hard to sell it because, quite frankly, when he gets his next commission check in a day or so he plans to buy it for himself. "It's one of those lots I can hold for a year, resell and make a nice profit on."

If the whole performance has been credible, you may find that you can make up your mind to buy it after all!

The "Inside" Price Ploy

This one is crude and obvious, and if you fall for it you deserve little sympathy. In its simplest application you get the tour and at some point, if the salesman thinks you are having doubts, he will look around furtively, then let you in on a secret.

"I'm not supposed to tell a customer this, but the prices in this unit are going up one thousand dollars a lot next Wednesday. If you are interested at all, you can save a thousand dollars (or *make* a thousand) by giving me a returnable deposit on it now."

Obvious as it is, the ploy works and many a raw land salesman has used that hustle to surround himself with contracts signed by fools who, from their money had soon been parted!

The Hotel Rumor Ploy

This is a variation of the price ploy and if a customer can prove that it has been worked on him, he can sue and collect damages and probably do others a service by putting the promoter out of business.

Prerequisites for this deception are impressive color brochures, elaborate artist's renderings of proposed improvements, a "resounding" corporate name on whose board sit some well-known local citizens of sterling character—and a salesman who is absolutely devoid of conscience.

The ploy is usually worked on prospects for commercial property such as a small businessman in his own hometown—information that is easily obtained from the questionnaire the victim is usually asked to fill out.

After a glowing account of all the proposed amenities that are planned—usually represented as "already funded and contracts are let"—the "pigeon" is shown a piece of raw desert or swampland. On the rendering it is located in the heart of "the downtown area."

At this point the salesman, wishing to dispel the very real vision of rattlesnakes or alligators, pulls from his briefcase a worn newspaper clipping bearing a recent date—perhaps no more than two months past.

There, beneath the headline, is a four-column reproduction of the architect's concept of the new 400-room Hiatus House Hotel that the international chain is soon to erect just a block away! Very impressive indeed! But the whole thing is a phony. The hotel chain may be real—or it may not exist, depending upon the guts of the promoter. The story was never run. It is a clever counterfeit of a newspaper page—masthead invariably missing—that has been prepared for the purpose of plucking a "pigeon" by hustling him in on the ground floor.

Fortunately, this bit of grand larceny is seldom tried anymore in so flagrant a form. But the "rumor ruse" has returned to take its place. Cautious con men have fallen back on one of the oldest time-tested tactics known to man. It would not surprise us if Egyptologists do not, some day, decode a newly discovered hieroglyphic that reads: "The *Daily Papyrus* learned today that Master Builder Upyr Ali, has purchased four hectares adjoining the Cheops Pyramid as a site for his new 100-tent Camel-tel. The rumor has touched off brisk speculation in sand lots."

There are many variations on these gambits. Their object is always the same—to "motivate" the buyer. This is usually accomplished by appealing to our very human avariciousness—at the bottom of which is an atavistic insecurity or need to guarantee our chances for survival.

There are very few creature-comfort problems that we will face in our later years that cannot be solved or at least assuaged by sufficient cash or liquid assets. It is this need that the clever salesman counts on exploiting one way or another. He knows that he will never meet a prospect who does not yearn to make some money—or more money. And if the salesman knows his sales psychology and he has even a passable product to sell, he'll make a very good living.

Some raw land salesmen make such a good living that they work only part of the year to keep from developing a tax problem. It is not uncommon for a skilled salesman with good "front window-dressing" at his disposal to make upward of $75,000 a year in commissions.

The "Endorsement" Ploy

Another frequently used device is the endorsement. But let us make it perfectly clear that in most cases it is used legitimately, and it is seldom used to deliberately mislead or misrepresent. The star "names" who front these promotions are generally too smart to permit themselves to be put in jeopardy through association with a questionable project. If they are not, then most assuredly their lawyers and managers are.

The name "Roy Rogers" lends undeniable appeal to a high desert region known as Apple Valley in Southern California. Lawrence Welk and Art Linkletter are both "glamorous names" who have developed top-quality mobile home communities. So is Fess Parker who, forgive us, has proved to be a "Boone" to mobile park development in the Santa Barbara area.

Bob Hope has lent his name and his millions to some excellent developments. Kino Springs, a superb second-home recreational project not far from Nogales, Arizona, makes good use of the fact that its clubhouse was once the elegant residence of movie star Stewart Granger, most of whose ranch the developer acquired. Lake California, a recreational development on the Sacramento River in Northern California, advertises itself as being in "Glenn Ford Country." In Arizona we saw a promotion that advertised itself as being "adjacent to the John Wayne Ranch." In this case we rather imagine the promoter is happier about his location than the star may be unless, of course, there is actually some business connection. And let's not forget Chet Huntley and *Big Sky!*

Often, as indicated earlier, these star "names" will have made a substantial personal investment in a development. Most buyers who have chosen to bask in reflected glory are well satisfied with their purchases, and not a few have made substantial profits.

The various ploys used to motivate the buyer are standard sales tactics. Except for those that are rank misrepresentations, there is little essential ethical difference between them and the hard-sell commercials that assail you on the TV screen (usually during the dinner hour when you should be relaxing or unwinding from the pressures of the day).

In essence the land salesman who conjures up a golden future for you in Heavenly Acres is far more humane than the classy, cello-voiced announcer or the velvet-voiced "aren't we fortunate" actress who would set us to worrying about the danger symptoms of "scaly lesions that may foretell a tragic skin disease" or those "nagging personal itches" that can back us up the wall. Of course, we are not likely to get either of these ailments unless the commercial barrages get us so uptight that we become susceptible.

In previous books we have done our share of exposing the rawest of the raw land deals. And where we find other such deals that seem to offer little or no hope of panning out within a couple of decades, we will continue to warn readers against them.

But strangely enough, very few big land promoters really deserve to be "tarred with a rough brush" on that score. Their projects may be premature and they may remain so for some years, but there are many instances where time has proved the visionary land developer was correct. We can think of at least a half dozen well-planned developments that would have been well timed had there not been a recession.

In the Pacific Northwest and in Southern California more than one development went through hard times when the aerospace slump came. Some failed. Those who were able to hang on are in business again, and sales are exceeding their original expectations—five years late!

In and around Atlanta, Georgia, and in other southern centers that have attracted new industry, good developments are doing well. In the South the same high-pressure tactics are used effectively, but somehow innate southern graciousness and the slower tempo makes them seem downright pleasant—at least to these "Westerners." Southern salesmen may invite you to "set down and reason together" over a julep instead of zonking you over rough desert roads at speeds that make that movie cartoon about the roadrunner bird look like Leadfoot Charlie.

If you have read the sensational news stories that purport to expose the unethical practices of land developers, you may get the impression that all developers reap exhorbitant profits. Not true.

A number of highly advertised developments that use high-pressure methods to merchandise their lots are not actually cleaning up at your expense. If they are putting in the amenities they have promised, they had better have bought their raw land cheap.

Streets, curbs, sidewalks, underground utilities, sewerage treatment plants, golf courses, clubhouses, canals and marinas do not come cheap. A developer may buy his raw land for less than $200 an acre. In some areas he will have paid a lot more. But even at the most advantageous borrowing rate, he will have committed himself to spend millions before he can expect to develop a cash flow from sales that will amortize his debts and produce some profit. If he has kept his promises to improve the property, he is justified in asking a good price for the finished lots.

In short, there are good and bad butchers and bakers and candlestick makers—and land developers. The hope of this work, *Land Investment, U.S.A.,* is that it will show the reader how to tell the difference.

21.
Power—Progress or Panic?

Benjamin Disraeli said, "Man is not the creature of circumstances. Circumstances are the creatures of men."

Though millions still do not acknowledge it, we Americans now face a crisis imposed upon ourselves by our insistence upon endless creature comforts and by our indifference to the public welfare. That crisis threatens to radically alter our cherished American life-style. And still, few people actually believe that.

We are among those fortunate writers who find most of their works being published. But during the past two years nine publishers have politely expressed their disinterest in a book dealing with the impending energy crisis, its cause and its probable cure.

We were tempted to respond with an appropriate jeremiad:

> *Hear now this, foolish people, and without understanding: Which have eyes, and see not, which have ears and hear not!*

But in the end we knew that the universality of the crisis would be made painfully clear when our publishing friends found themselves with furnaces that heat not; lamps that light not; and cars that run not.

Somehow, it must be made evident that not one of those possibilities is a figment of some public relation man's "diabolical" imagination. Neither is it a tactic in a secret plan to panic us into endangering the entire nation for the sake of stockholders' and bondholders' profit. The energy crisis is a cold, stark possibility. Indeed, if we do not adopt a realistic attitude toward it, that crisis is an *imminent probability.*

At present, domestically produced oil and gas provide about 70 percent of America's energy requirements.

In just twelve years we will be forced to import more than 50 percent of our oil and gas needs, unless we can acknowledge the validity of the problem we have all drifted into together and agree on some practical compromises.

The United States of America has only 6 percent of the world's population; but we use 33 percent of the world's available energy.

In 1972 our trade deficit was the worst in the nation's history—*$6.4 billion!*

By 1980 we could suffer a trade deficit of *$18 billion in imported crude oil and liquid natural gas alone!*

The political consequences could be profound. One aspect of the problem was voiced by an economist who said, "We might be forced to desert the Israeli temple for the Arabian tent." Crude though it be, the man stated a geopolitical truth.

Who can predict the consequences of a 50 percent—or larger—dependency on the Near East for oil and liquified natural gas shipped to us over thousands of miles of open sea in *militarily vulnerable* supertankers?

Does anyone with even a "five-watt glimmer" of political awareness and an elementary understanding of human nature think that even the most "friendly" Arab nations would refrain from using that sort of economic leverage to put us over an oil barrel—if they felt they could get away with it?

Even if they resisted the temptation and reversed their entire historical behavior pattern, what would prevent some other power with sociopolitical and economic ambitions from blackmailing us at sea?

Ridiculous? Ask the Pacific tuna fleet! Ask the Gulf shrimp fleet! These documented "incidents" have long since proved that our government has chosen to pay ransom rather than risk a world conflagration. Should not we ask at what point does "moral responsibility" become *immoral irresponsibility?*

But we're off the point, in danger of starting that factual book on our energy crisis that some still seem to regard as fiction. This particular book is about land investment and the relevant point is this: *We may find that development of valuable property that should be used for residences, manufacturing and recreation cannot be utilized because, quite simply, there will not be enough electrical generating capacity or sufficient fuel to provide basic services.*

That possibility is being widely pooh-poohed despite incontrovertible evidence that such shortages already exist.

In the District of Columbia, the Washington Gas and Light Company is reported to have stopped accepting new industrial customers until new capacity can be developed.

An operating official of the Southern California Edison Company admitted to us that unless they can reach some acceptable compromise with the opponents of nuclear generating plants, the company may be unable to supply electricity to new industry: This comes at a time when national needs have made California the number one industrial state in the Union.

It takes very little imagination to visualize what such shortages can mean in potential new jobs that will not materialize as the problem spreads. Certainly it must be clear that the new housing needed for those workers would also be scratched. In fact, the Southern California Edison Company, like many other private and publicly owned utility companies, is already experiencing difficulty in providing services to the suburbs that have sprung up in Orange County to meet the influx of new families resulting from the state's industrial growth.

"Our reserve generating capacity is already at the danger point," the official admitted. From personal investigation we know that the same situation exists in many areas along the eastern seaboard.

Six New England states struggle through the winter on the narrowest possible margin of energy reserves. One executive in Boston said, "We are operating on a day-to-day basis now—and have been for the past three years."

Several large gas companies, among them the Tennessee Gas Transmission Company, are reported to have notified their customers that they can no longer supply service beyond the quantites presently being used. In effect, this says, "Do not expand your businesses because we cannot provide you with gas."

Schools were closed in Denver, Colorado, during the winter of 1972-1973 to conserve dwindling fuel reserves. In Des Moines, Iowa, hospitals were given priority in fuel deliveries as thousands of home owners were forced to conserve drastically.

In Mississippi, West Virginia and Illinois, factories were forced to close for brief periods when fuel supplies were exhausted. In the winter of 1972-1973, shortages of jet fuel forced the cancellation of scores of passenger flights originating at John F. Kennedy Airport in New York. Other flights, normally nonstop, were forced to make intermediate fuel stops.

How is the emergency being met now? Belatedly, the Office of Emergency Preparedness in Washington has increased oil import quotas, thus moving us another step toward critical dependency on foreign energy sources. And all of this is reputed to be part of some "dire plot" on the part of the utility companies to force us to accept nuclear fission, high-sulfur domestic oil and dirty soft coal as energy sources "because there's more profit in it."

Anyone who thinks twice must see the sheer lunacy of such allegations. If these companies are really "profit hungry," the worst possible thing they can do is operate in a "panic configuration."

We are not apologists. And we are not havoc criers. We have no doubt that the same technological genius that has made the United States the master of space will also work its miracles to provide us with clean, new energy sources. The trouble we face in the immediate future stems from the fact that we have not built up sufficient lead time. We have been so occupied with our prodigal—indeed, *profligate*—use of cheap electricity and gas that we have ignored the problem with "ears that hear not" and "eyes that see not."

We have been unwilling to deprive ourselves, or even to limit our use, of these conveniences because we have learned to take for granted blessings that people in other countries gladly sacrifice for.

The conservationists are right when they charge that we often waste our energy. But they are wrong when they contend that if we just ration our use of gas and electricity the shortage will disappear.

Industry studies show that if we do limit ourselves to the irreducible minimum usage of electricity and natural gas, the savings would be only 20 percent of our present usage. Worth doing, certainly, but not enough by *five times*.

There is no doubt that our houses can be made more efficient through better insulation. In newer developments they can be designed and positioned to take advantage of solar heat during the day. Appliances can be made more efficient. So can furnaces. New lighting techniques can provide more efficient illumination in homes, offices and factories, and do it with less wattage. Use habits can be changed so that fewer appliances are run at peak load times, and they can be run less often.

A number of industries, including the Aluminum Company of America, one of the nation's largest users of electrical energy,

have devised power-conserving systems that make their manufacturing processes still more efficient.

DuPont has taken the lead in applying new energy-saving
procedures in its own plants and in a score of other companies.
The energy savings are said to be as much as 15 percent; and at
least 60 percent of the improvement has been effected without
expensive remodeling.

Undoubtedly there is a "light at the end of the energy
tunnel" too. But it is going to take until the turn of the new
century to solve the problem, even if we initiate immediately a
new crash program of research and development directed
toward generating new sources of energy and devising more
efficient ways to employ them.

In the meantime, it makes good sense for a land investor,
whether he is interested in raw acreage or improved property, to
take a long, hard look at the prospects for an adequate supply
of energy, whatever its source, to maintain his home and a
normal expansion of his business.

"How can we get such information?" asked a friend who has
a sixty-acre parcel of undeveloped land in escrow on which he
hopes to develop a recreation vehicle resort.

"By calling the local gas and electric company and asking
them flat out," we replied.

We have asked the same questions in Florida, in Oregon, in
Nevada and in California, and never once have we gotten an
evasive answer. The utility companies are required by law to
provide service if it is physically possible. They have neither the
time nor the inclination for "double talk." A prospective investor may rely absolutely on the answers he receives.

So do not hesitate to ask. *By doing so you may become part
of the solution* instead of part of the problem.

22.
Before You Sign

The rising clamor for more open space will motivate the politicians to implement the condemnation and purchase of hundreds of thousands of acres to be left in "green belt" areas.

As this land is set aside it will have to be paid for from the public funds replenished by added taxes or usage fees, or by developers who find new zoning now requires so much open space per hundred units of dwelling.

Whichever method is used—and both will be—the taxpayer and the new home buyer will ultimately get the bill.

As the supply of buildable land diminishes under new restrictions, the land that is zoned for dwellings of various sorts, and for the commercial enterprises that must service such communities, will increase in value. The basic law of the marketplace again—the law of supply and demand.

Since we have seen that even if we achieve zero population growth, our numbers will continue to increase well into the twenty-first century, it must be apparent that "people pressure" will continue to exert its value-boosting effect on good land.

This is a deliberate oversimplification because by now, hopefully, the reader will have understood the basic complications inherent in the problem. The conclusion, then, is that good land, well used, is still our best and most secure investment.

Remember—where individual parcels of land are concerned, there is no such thing as a "sure thing." After the potential investor has honestly answered the question, "Why do I want to invest in land?" and goes looking for the lot, the parcel or the acreage that suits his purpose, he will still have to ask all of those other questions that we have posed in the various chapters.

Remember, too, that price does not always reflect value. Indeed, where prices are arbitrarily increased by the developer as part of his sales ploy, the tactic may decrease the actual value of the property, especially if the development is economically unanchored and if it is so large that it will accommodate tens of thousands of people and will take the developer decades to sell. There are many such that are well advertised.

One developer in the Southwest testified that he did not expect his community to be fully populated until the year 2000! That, he said, was why he was taking his time about putting in many of the "improvements" he had been advertising as investment attractions.

It would be unfair to imply that any increase in price initiated by the developer is a "hyp" tactic—an artificial injection of "value" to panic prospects into signing while the "introductory" price is still in effect.

We have visited many excellent developments where the prices of comparable property in subsequent units have been increased for two perfectly legitimate reasons: Rising construction costs have forced the developer to pay more for improvements; and rising values in the property already sold and built upon justify the increase on a sound economic basis. *Lakeway* near Austin, Texas, is a good example of legitimate upward market pressure.

All good land holds a profit potential if it meets the criteria outlined in the foregoing chapters. As we have said repeatedly: If buyers will reckon the pleasure they and their families derive from well-chosen land investments—particularly where second-home recreational land is concerned—then, in the abstract sense of the word, it is correct for them to conclude that they have made a "killing."

One last observation. Buyers, particularly inexperienced ones, tend to be a bit apologetic about asking questions of the seller. *That is a serious mistake.* Remember, if you are a potential buyer, you wield the power even if you do not have the cash. In fact, many sellers prefer a buyer with good credit. A long-term financing deal earns him a lot more dollars in interest. In effect, he is making substantially more profit on the land. So the sellers, whether they are owners or brokers, are anxious to meet you. Do not let their assured front intimidate you. A good salesman maintains what Chicago insurance tycoon W. Clement Stone calls *PMA—Positive Mental Attitude.* And it works—both ways!

So keep a positive mental attitude about those questions you must demand honest answers to before you sign a commitment.

To borrow a line from an old English music hall song:

> Listen well my little beauty,
> I'm the bloke who's got the "booty"
> And to me, you'll do your duty
> By not forgetting that booty's the boss!

*51. The "theme symbol" of McCulloch Oil Corporation's newest spectac-
ular planned community since Arizona's Lake Havasu City. Fountain Hills,
not far from Phoenix and Scottsdale, is near a chain of four recreational
lakes, part of the Salt River Project. A fifth lake is proposed right next
door. Fountain Hills is planned for an eventual population of 70,000
persons or about 6 to the acre. Old cities generally contain 40 to 60
persons to the acre. Ten thousand square feet is the minimum residential
lot. Prices start from $8,000. All of the standard amenities are present.*

52. *From five miles distant, an incredible sight . . . a five-hundred-foot fountain of freshwater rising from the floor of a desert! Who would dream up a fountain higher than the Washington Monument? Who else but "those wonderful folks who 'gave' us The London Bridge" at Lake Havasu City, the McCulloch Oil Corporation.*

Index